Reading and Writing
Before School

# Reading and Writing Before School

FELICITY HUGHES

with an Introduction by GLENN DOMAN

THE READING REVOLUTION—at home and at school—based on Glenn Doman's *Teach Your Baby To Read*

Jonathan Cape Thirty Bedford Square London

FIRST PUBLISHED 1971
© 1971 BY FELICITY HUGHES

JONATHAN CAPE LTD, 30 BEDFORD SQUARE, LONDON WCI

ISBN 0 224 61901 2

PRINTED IN GREAT BRITAIN
BY EBENEZER BAYLIS AND SON LIMITED
THE TRINITY PRESS, WORCESTER, AND LONDON
BOUND BY G. AND J. KITCAT LTD, LONDON

# Contents

# Introduction by Glenn Doman

This brilliant book by a brilliant mother and teacher is worth many times the price and the time it takes to read it.

For twenty years and more I have been persuaded that mothers are the most maligned of people. Among professional people who deal with mothers and children, there is an unspoken law which says that all mothers are idiots and that the truth is not in them.

The fact is that mothers know more about their own kids than anyone else alive and I am scared to death that we professionals are going to talk them out of their maternal instincts and bully them out of their innate good sense.

Felicity Hughes, who wrote this book, is a mother and one doesn't have to read very far in this book of hers to know that, thank the Lord, she is deeply emotionally involved with her children. What is more, nobody is about to beat her out of her opinions.

Felicity Hughes is also a teacher and one doesn't have to read far in her book to know that as a teacher she is as deeply emotionally involved with everybody else's child as she is with her own and we can thank the good Lord for that as well.

Mrs Hughes's book tells us how to teach babies to read

and to write and a good deal more about how to deal with babies and tiny children.

This is a joyful book full of equal parts of bubbling happiness and good sense, as all books about dealing with children should be.

It is at once high as a kite and down to earth, and that's elegant too.

I agree with virtually all, but not quite all, that Felicity Hughes has to say. My only disagreement with her comes in the area of phonetics and it is difficult for me to understand how so bright a girl, as she obviously is, could have fallen for that series of grunts, surds and sibilants called phonemes and morphemes from which the people called linguists have constructed an empire. I believe that Mrs Hughes taught her children to read despite rather than because of phonetics, as a product of her brilliance as a teacher and mother.

She is alert and clever enough to make even the phonetics jargon sound almost plausible. Still when I think about it, I suppose there is nobody I agree with entirely, so it is not surprising that I don't agree with everything Felicity Hughes says.

I believe that this book is a must for mothers who enjoy their children and who want to give them the best opportunity for coping with the incredibly complex and not altogether rational world they are about to inherit. I advise them to skip the section on phonetics and to enjoy the rest of the book as immensely as they are certain to do.

There is one thing on which I agree entirely with Mrs Hughes, something which emerges on every page although she never says it. That is this: almost everybody loves kids, almost nobody respects them for being the magnificent and potential geniuses they all are. Compared to kids, adults are hopelessly retarded. I have vast respect for children and so does Mrs Hughes.

No mother who reads this book carefully or even lightly can fail to be a better mother for having done so, whether in the end she decides to teach her baby to read and write or whether she does not.

GLENN DOMAN

# Acknowledgments

To Dr Glenn Doman, without whose book *Teach Your Baby To Read*, my children would never have learned to read at home, nor would this book have been written.

To Susanne Langer, whose book *Philosophy in a New Key* gave me an excited interest in the workings of language.

To Methuen Ltd, for permission to quote from Desmond Vesey's translation of *The Life of Galileo* by Bertolt Brecht.

To Heinemann Educational Books Ltd, for permission to quote from *The Basic Colour Factor Guide* by Seton Pollock.

To Wills and Hepworth Ltd, for permission to identify the Key Words used in my book as being taken from *The Ladybird Key Words Reading Scheme*.

To my family, for putting up with me while I hatched a book: my husband, for his unfailing interest and willingness to discuss each new idea as it emerged; my father, for his interest; my mother, herself a former infants' teacher, who shared my growing enthusiasm for Doman's ideas; my sister, who seized on Doman's discoveries about large print to help backward Jamaican teenagers to read; my cousin Margaret Connor, who tracked down vitally useful background information; my children, who took to reading like ducks to water.

FOR MY MOTHER

# Author's Foreword

'Real' language is spoken language, heard and used. Children learn 'real' language at home, by hearing it and using it. Much later, when they are ready for 'formal' education, they are told that people have invented written symbols for 'real' language, and that if they try hard enough, they can learn to read and to write.

For centuries we have believed that this is the way things are, and so for centuries children have learned to read and write in the way I have described. But some years ago, an American specialist in the problems of brain damage looked closely at our language universe, and it seemed to him that this was not the way things were at all. It seemed to him that written language was real language, and spoken language was real language, and that a knowledge of either one did not depend on a knowledge of the other.

If Dr Doman is right, then he offers as radical a challenge to educational thinking today as Copernicus and Galileo offered to the religious thinking of their day, when they took a closer look at the Ptolemaic universe, and suggested that that was not the way things were either.

I have written this book in an effort to come to grips with some of the implications of Dr Doman's theory. For, if he is right, then this must mean not only that babies can learn to read as easily, as quickly and in the same way as they learn to understand speech; it must also mean that we need to re-examine all the assumptions on which reading instruction is based, at school as well as at home.

Because Dr Doman is primarily concerned with the human brain, and not with language as such, nor with 'formal' education at all, there are one or two gaps in his theory. As a teacher and mother with an interest in the way language works, I think I have been able to fill in those gaps, and to see that not only reading, but phonetics, writing and spelling must find new positions in the universe which Dr Doman has set spinning. And in this new language universe, deaf babies may be able to find a place almost as easily as hearing children.

I believe that we shall gradually come to take it for granted that children should learn to read, to turn written words into sounds, to write and to spell at home, as naturally as they now learn to hear and speak. My book, which grew out of *Teach Your Baby To Read*, by Glenn Doman, is for parents who want this to happen in their homes.

But as it will obviously be many long years before every five-year-old goes to school fully literate, my book is also an attempt to bring the Doman revolution into the class-room.

There are numerous references in my text to reading books I would recommend. These are listed on p. 163 in a short Bibliography. Further useful titles in both Ladybird Books and the Beginner Books Series have become available since my book was written.

F.H.

*Sagredo*: But the moon cannot be an earth with mountains and valleys, any more than the earth can be a planet.

*Galileo*: The moon can be an earth with mountains and valleys, and the earth *can* be a planet ... It shines in the same way as the moon shines. Both planets are illuminated by the sun – that is why they shine. What the moon is to us, we are to the moon ...

*Sagredo*: That would mean that there is no difference between the moon and the earth.

*Galileo*: Evidently not.

BRECHT: *The Life of Galileo*

# PART ONE

Shapes, Sounds and Symbols

# 1

## The Doman Revolution

'Oh Mummy! *Don't* put out the light yet — I've only got three more pages to go!' Helen, at bed-time. Younger sister Gwynneth, predictable echo, only bossier, chips in. '*Mummy.* I'm just in the middle of reading a story. *Wait.*' A typical bed-time in a typical English home. The only thing that makes this one slightly different is that Helen is five, Gwynneth is three.

Anita comes from New Delhi. She is four years old. Until a few months ago, she spoke only Hindi, and could understand no English. Now she has finished seven simple English readers and an alphabet book, and has an English reading vocabulary of about 300 words. She can easily prove that she understands these words by touching some flowers, for example, when she is shown that word. Her English speaking vocabulary is growing too.

Elizabeth is five. She lives in New Zealand and recently started school. When the beginners were tested, the surprised head-teacher discovered that Elizabeth had a reading age of nine.

In America, a one-year-old brain-injured boy picks up a book and reads through the pages with obvious delight.

These are only examples. The list could be extended

indefinitely. But who are the children, and why can they read so easily? Are they freaks, examples of extraordinary intellectual ability? Or, if they are not, have they been subjected to some dreadful techniques which have forced them to develop prematurely?

The children are not freaks. Nobody has forced them to do anything. What has happened to them is something very simple; it could happen to any human baby, anywhere.

*These children have been helped to use their eyes as well as their ears.*

A human baby of ten months is a pretty helpless creature. He cannot walk, or even stand unaided. He cannot speak.

His father picks him up, laughing at him.

'Where's Mummy?' he asks.

The baby's face breaks into a grin. He cranes around in his father's arms, looking towards the woman in the doorway and gurgling cheerfully.

'You see,' she says, as she comes to take him, 'he does understand.'

The baby is an average human baby. Helpless he may be, but a pattern of trivial sounds, carried to his brain through his ears, has conveyed to him a clear meaning. He can distinguish a certain arrangement of nasal murmuring noises from many other sound patterns, even those which resemble it quite closely. And he knows that this particular pattern means the human being at the centre of his world. The sound 'Mummy' summons up in his mind an image of his mother, and recognizing her footsteps at the door, he does all he can to point her out.

The ability of a human baby to understand and distinguish various sound patterns in this way is an ability that many of us have taken for granted for too long.

Glenn Doman is an American specialist in the treatment of brain-injured children. Several years ago, he stopped taking for granted this human ability to hear meanings through sounds. He had discovered that human babies of one year old or less could be taught to read. The more he thought about it, the less surprising this discovery became. For if an arbitrary collection of sounds, formed into a word, could convey a meaning to a one-year-old, why should it not be possible for an arbitrary collection of shapes to do the same?

After many years of observation and experiment, Dr Doman recorded his findings in a book, *Teach Your Baby To Read*, and set in motion the Doman revolution. The book is mainly a presentation of facts about the reading abilities of very young children, facts which are startling enough in themselves. But at the heart of these facts lies an idea which is even more startling, which may eventually re-shape almost all our former notions about the education of young children, at home or at school, the education of brain-injured children and the education of the deaf.

The idea is this: that a written word is *exactly* comparable to a spoken word.

Dr Doman's book is based on a very simple comparison of spoken and written words. It is so simple that hardly anyone has thought of it before:

What is a spoken word?

A spoken word has a meaning, and it is made up of sounds. Take it to bits and examine each sound in turn, and the meaning has vanished. Put the sounds together again — and the word is something much more than the sum of its parts. What we are aware of when we hear a spoken word is the meaning coming through the sounds. In fact, we are hardly aware of the *sounds* at all.

With some mysterious ability which we human beings possess, we have taken a collection of sounds and made it into something new—a symbol. The symbol is nothing in itself. But it is meaningful because of what it represents.

And even babies can understand what spoken symbols represent.

What is a *written* word?

A written word has a meaning, and it is a collection of shapes. Take it to bits and examine each shape in turn, and the meaning has vanished. Put the shapes back together again—and the word is something much more than the sum of its parts. What we are aware of when we see a written word is the meaning coming through the shapes. In fact, we are hardly aware of the *shapes* at all.

Just as we have been able to transform a collection of trivial sounds, making it into a symbol, so we have been able to transform a collection of trivial shapes, making that into a symbol as well. The symbol is nothing in itself. But it is meaningful because of what it represents.

*And even babies can understand what written symbols represent.*

Glenn Doman's theory runs like this: when a symbol reaches the brain, the brain understands it in terms of what it represents. And whether such a symbol reaches the brain via the eyes or via the ears makes no difference whatever to the way the brain interprets that symbol. Reading, therefore, and hearing speech, are closely similar functions of the brain. One is not dependent on the other. The difference between reading and hearing is no more than the difference between the sense organs through which the symbols are transmitted.

The first question we must ask about such a startling theory is not: 'What shall we do with it?' but: 'Is it *true*?'

There are two ways of tackling this question. One way is to examine language itself and to see whether its various forms with their various functions can, logically, fit the comparison which Doman has made. In my final chapter, I hope to show not only that they can and do fit, but also that Doman's theory sheds new light on the whole structure of language.

The second way is to ask: 'What follows for the human beings using language? What, if Doman is right, will they be capable of achieving?' And then we must find out if these things do, in fact, happen. Dr Doman has tackled the question in this way, and has accumulated a great mass of evidence to support his ideas. For example, it follows that if the brain is doing exactly the same thing when it understands written words as when it understands spoken words, *a child must be able to read as easily as he can understand the words he hears.*

As soon as he shows that he understands the spoken word 'mummy', for instance, he must be capable of reading it.

Doman has found out that babies *can* understand written words when they are beginning to understand spoken words.

It follows, next, that reading must be *easier* than speaking.

When a child understands a word, either spoken or written, he is doing *one* thing – interpreting. But when he reproduces a spoken word meaningfully, he must first be able to understand that spoken word, and then he must work out how to direct his vocal chords to make the proper sounds.

Doman has found out that babies who are exposed to written words as well as spoken words do, in fact, learn to read many words before they can say them. (He discovered this by saying to the child: 'Show me the word that says –' instead of: 'What does this say?')

We may ask: 'If all this is true, why don't children learn

to read naturally, just as they learn to understand speech?'
The answer is very simple. We expose a child to meaningful
speech almost without thinking about it, because we are
continually using it in his presence. We don't expose him to
written words, because it means making special materials,
and this doesn't occur to us. We teach him spoken language
quite casually; we have to teach him to read *deliberately*.

But the main reason that he doesn't pick up reading by
himself is that even large book print, as Doman discovered,
is too small for a baby to read at first. When he is exposed to
meaningful words in huge letters, he learns to read them very
easily.

You can test for yourself how much easier it is to recognize and learn big words than small ones. Choose a page
of ordinary sized print, and turn it upside-down. Now you
are seeing words as a beginning reader sees them—as pure
arrangements of shapes, without any particular correlation
with sounds. Don't try to *say* these words, or understand
them, but try to pick out two identical ones. The smaller the
print, the more difficult this is. Take a child's book with the
largest print you can find and do the same. It is much easier
to recognize identical words. This experiment will also help
you to see that each word has its own individual look, a
total appearance which emerges when its constituent letters
are seen as a combined whole. Again, the bigger the print,
the more striking each individual form.

If a letter in a word is altered, so changing the total form,
the meaning alters likewise. If a sound in a spoken word is
altered, so changing the total heard impression, the meaning
of the word alters in the same way. It is no more surprising
that children should be able to detect and understand such
slight differences in the words they *see*, than that they
should be able to detect and understand them in the words

they *hear*. And the bigger the print, the clearer these alterations in visual form become.

(We may even find that many apparent cases of 'dislexia', word blindness, respond to a large enough increase in the size of the print. My sister was giving remedial reading lessons to hard-core non-readers who were twelve and thirteen years old. She got hold of a Doman kit for other purposes, and as an experiment, used some of the big word cards in her reading class. At the end of half an hour, two of three children who had not been able to read a word until then could both read about six words each, although they were still unable to recognize these same words in a book. This is an isolated instance, but I think that the possibilities it raises could bear investigation.)

If Doman's comparison between spoken and written language is accurate, *it is likely that the only reason a child finds reading more 'difficult' than understanding speech is that it is more difficult for* us *to make the proper materials available.*

We can go on from here to draw some analogies. We know that if a child is born deaf, it is important to teach him to understand spoken language, in one way or another, as soon as possible (using hearing-aids, or gestures and pictures to teach lip-reading, and so on). The older he gets before we make a beginning, the more difficult it is for him to learn.

So from this we should expect to find that children who do not begin learning to *read* before five, will learn to read more slowly than they learned to hear.

They do.

Then we should expect to find that children learn to read *more easily* the younger they are. Doman has found out that a child can learn to read more easily at two than three, more easily at three than four, more easily at four than five.

It also follows from Doman's theory that it should be possible to teach deaf children to understand written language without any reference to spoken language, and of course this is often done. Doman himself has taught dozens of deaf children to read.

It looks as if the Doman theory of reading, revolutionary though it is, may be here to stay.

And now we are landed with the question of what to do with it.

Shall we do as Doman suggests, and teach our babies to read at home?

People who recommend early reading seem to run into all kinds of opposition straight away. There are the educationists who believe that reading readiness is almost a matter of biological development, 'part of the time-table of growing up'.* They say that a child should learn to read when he indicates that he is ready, and that left to himself he is not normally ready before the age of five or six. There are the teachers who believe that a child learning to read is also learning *how* to learn, and that if he reads 'too soon' he will do so 'only at the expense of far more basic attitudes to learning and thinking'. There are the teachers who are afraid that methods used by parents may conflict with those of the school. And there are many people who think that it is cruel to inflict 'formal learning' on a pre-schooler.

But if Doman is right about the similarity between written and spoken words, all such criticisms fall to the ground. Reading readiness may be a matter of biological development—as long as the print remains small. It is not that a child is *intellectually* unable to read before the age of five or six; merely that it is not until he is *about* five or six that

* All unidentified quotes in this chapter are taken from *Success Before Six*, a series on early education published by the *Sunday Times* in March 1968.

his visual sense is sufficiently mature for him to begin to discriminate between words in ordinary book print. Of course, the solution is not to make him wait until he is five or six before he begins to read. All we need to do is to make the print big enough for him to see. Once a baby is accustomed to understanding Doman's enormous words, he can rapidly learn to distinguish between words in smaller print.

To say that it is wrong to show a child written words in a meaningful way before he has told us that he wants to read, is like saying that it is wrong to talk to a child before he has indicated that he wants to hear. Left to himself, when would he guess that his ears could convey a whole world of exciting meanings? At four? At five? At six?

And if the brain is doing exactly the same thing whether it reads or whether it hears, then learning to read *cannot* happen 'at the expense of far more basic attitudes to learning and thinking' – unless we feel that the brain shouldn't be engaged in interpreting symbols at all. In which case, again, we had better stop talking to our children before they are five years old!

We can sympathize, though, with people who hate the idea of subjecting small children to 'formal education'. If parents are going to spend long hours putting their children through the worst kind of classroom drills, then all the reading ability in the world is not going to be worth the cost. But Doman has shown us that learning to read does not have to be like that at all – that it can involve more natural, loving communication between a child and his mother than all his other play.

For a child whose mother uses Doman's methods, learning to read *is* play. The first word he reads is the name of the most important person in his world – 'mummy'. It is a huge, exciting red shape on a white background.* He sees it for only a few seconds at a time, associated with his mother's closeness and loving interest in what he is doing, and associated also with the sound 'mummy'. The word is briefly presented three times during a session of no more than five minutes, and this five-minute session is repeated about five times during the day.

The following day, at the third session, the mother shows the word and asks her child what it says. Almost certainly, he will reply 'mummy', and be greeted with praise and hugs, but if he hesitates for long, his mother simply tells him 'mummy' again, happily.

When he is certain of 'mummy', the card is put aside and he learns 'daddy' in the same way. Only then does he see the two words together, and learns to discriminate between them.

This method of presentation makes full use of the latest findings in child psychology and patterns of learning. The sessions are short, and so the child doesn't grow bored. The sessions are repeated at intervals, so that what is learned sinks in for a while, and is then reinforced before it can be forgotten. This is particularly important for the early sessions. If they were all clumped together in periods of thirty minutes or more, and not repeated for the rest of the day, learning would be irksome and far less rapid.

Doman maintains, rightly it seems to me, that the foundations of reading are: (1) the ability to understand an isolated word, and (2) the ability to discriminate between two words. His method solidly establishes these foundations, devoting more time and care to their development than any other teaching method I know.

* See Doman's book. The first two words, 'mummy' and 'daddy', are printed on white card in red letters about 2½ inches high.

Once these foundations are laid, the mother builds up a reading vocabulary which represents her child's familiar world and interests. His rate of learning progresses rapidly. He may begin by learning one word a day, but within months he can be absorbing as many as ten new words a day. His mother introduces sentences when she feels he is ready, and these sentences build up, page by page, into his first book.

This approach has little in common with 'formal' education, which usually involves too much testing. Testing in turn involves anxiety, pressure, sometimes a sense of failure. If this is what early reading means, then those who love children are right to disapprove. But Doman's approach concentrates almost entirely on *teaching*, and cuts testing to the minimum. A mother 'tests' her child only when she is as certain as she can be that he knows the word anyway. If he doesn't, she simply reads it for him again. If she finds that her child does not like to be tested, or does not respond, she can even dispense with testing altogether. She can go ahead and present written language to her baby as naturally and as meaningfully as she uses speech. She does not need to worry about whether or not he is responding, just as she goes on talking to him without stopping to find out if he can understand everything she says. *For as she talks to him, he learns to understand.*

She can show him a few word cards each day, and read them to him, introducing new ones at intervals. She can take these words from simple books in big, clear print, and read the books to her baby fairly slowly, pointing to each word as she reads. She can draw funny pictures for him, and put names on them. She can stick labels on objects in the house. Her child is taking it all in, whether or not he indicates that he can read the words. One day he will surprise her by reading a few sentences aloud.

There seems to be no reason why the mother of a deaf baby should not follow much the same approach. Perhaps we have not clearly recognized that since a deaf child can see so much better than he can hear, written language should be for him the chief means of understanding and organizing his world, just as spoken language is for a hearing child. A deaf baby should, if possible, learn to read when hearing children are learning to understand speech. Doman has discovered that a baby of ten months can be taught to read. It seems logical to suggest that the mother of a deaf baby, who is lucky enough to have had her child's hearing defect diagnosed in the first few months of his life, should make every effort to surround her child with meaningful written language, at least from ten months of age. So long as she concentrates on presenting written language meaningfully, rather than on testing her child's understanding of written words, she cannot possibly do him any harm. A limited amount of testing (seeing if the child can touch an object in response to the written word; or, later, carry out written instructions) will be helpful to the mother and amusing for the child.

Doman points out in his book that a child who cannot hear can learn to read, although he does not make clear how relevant his ideas are to the problem of deafness: 'If we had spoken in whispers while simultaneously writing words and sentences very large and distinct, very young children would be able to read but would be unable to understand verbal (i.e. spoken) language.' (*Teach Your Baby To Read*, pp. 26–7)

Written nouns can be made meaningful to a deaf child by being linked with concrete objects. Verbs can be made meaningful by being linked with actions. Adjectives can be linked with meaningful nouns, and then with big, or red, or heavy objects. Adverbs can be linked with verbs and then with particular kinds of actions (walking quickly, walking slowly, etc.). Other verbs, prepositions and conjunctions can be introduced in a sentence whose other words are already understood, and which describes a clearly obvious event. (The red book is *on* the table.)

To ensure that the written language presented to a deaf baby is natural and colloquial, rather than stilted and formal, a mother should talk to her baby frequently, as she would to a hearing child, paying careful attention to the kinds of phrases and sentences she naturally uses. If she has a tape recorder, it will be helpful if she records several of her own conversations with him. She can then listen to these on her own, listing the phrases and sentences that occur most frequently, and print them on a blackboard or a large piece of card so that she can later present them to her baby in the context of a similar situation. When she presents such a sentence, she should point to each word in fairly quick succession, so helping her baby to look at the words in a meaningful order. After a while, he will be able to take in the meaning of a short, familiar sentence in a single glance.

Of course, if the deaf baby can hear anything, with or without hearing-aids, he should be exposed to spoken language as well, separately, and in addition the written words he sees should be linked with spoken words so that he learns how they sound. They should likewise be linked with the natural, unexaggerated movements of his mother's lips as she utters them. But the baby does not have to hear the equivalent spoken words, or lip-read them, in order to *understand* the written forms.

Gradually, the pattern of understanding which a hearing child builds up as he learns to interpret sounds can be—and

3

often is—duplicated by the deaf child who is learning to interpret shapes.

For hearing children and non-hearing children alike, learning to understand written language need involve no pressure, no anxiety, no sense of failure. Nothing, in fact, but fun.

# 2

## The Function of Phonetics

Why have I used up space discussing an idea which has already been far better explained? (I need hardly say that my brief account is no substitute for Glenn Doman's exciting and moving book.)

There is one small catch in Doman's theory, and in order to deal with it, I needed to explain the theory as clearly as I could. The catch involves the thorny question which has plagued teachers of reading for many long years: phonetics.

Still the battle rages between the 'look-and-say' teachers and the 'alphabet-and-phonetics' teachers, and the pendulum swings between the two. At the moment we seem to be swinging back to the alphabet.

In its *Success Before Six* series, the *Sunday Times* declared: 'One thing had become certain, that the old "look-say" method—looking at words as a whole and parroting them out—which produced two generations of bad readers and bad spellers, was obviously ready for the scrap heap.'

Yet Glenn Doman's theory shows us that we had better dig up the 'whole word' approach from that scrap heap pretty damn fast. For if the brain understands written words in just the same way that it understands spoken words, then we should no more help a child to read by beginning with separate letters than we should help him to hear by beginning with separate sounds. (Do we point to a cat and say 'cu, a, tu'?!)

A written word is *more* than the sum of its shapes, and the 'look-and-say' theorists have known this instinctively without seeing it as clearly as Glenn Doman has done.

Doman has seen that understanding written words is exactly comparable to understanding spoken words. He points out that if we do not need to know phonetics in order to hear, then we do not need to know phonetics in order to read.

He is absolutely right.

'Look-and-say' works primarily, *not* because a child looks at a whole word and 'parrots out' the sound, but because he looks at a word and understands what the symbol represents. We should not really call it 'look-and-*say*' — it is 'look-and-*understand*'.

But then comes the catch. Doman implies that because we do not need to know phonetics in order to hear, and because we do not need to know phonetics in order to read, *then we do not need to know phonetics*.

And that is where he is wrong.

In his book, he refers to the battle between the 'look-and-say' approach and the 'alphabet-and-phonetics' approach as a peripheral battle. It is worse. It is a completely *idiotic* battle. It is like an argument between two teachers about educating a child, when one says: 'Well, *I* think we ought to teach him English.' And the other one says: 'Well *I* don't. *I* think we ought to teach him maths.'

The 'whole-word' teachers are quite right. *And the 'alphabet-and-phonetics' teachers are quite right.*

For a child needs to be able to see a word in *two* quite different ways, for *two* different purposes.

He needs to be able to see it as a meaningful symbol, so that he can *understand* it.

And he needs to be able to see it as an arrangement of sounds, so that he can *translate* it.

In order to see why this is so, let us take a clearer look at the relationship between written language and spoken language, in the light of Doman's theory. The first thing we can be clearer about is that a written word is not the symbol of a sound. That simple statement spells bloody revolution for almost all our former theories about how children learn to read. So let me repeat it.

*A written word is not the symbol of a sound.*

For centuries we have imposed unnecessary burdens on children learning to read because most of us have believed that written words *are* symbols of sounds. We have thought that we must first teach children to understand spoken words, and then we can teach them to read the written symbols for those sounds. The 'look-and-say' theorists think we should teach the sound for a whole word at once, and the alphabetic people think we should do it bit by bit.

But a written word is not the symbol of a sound any more than a spoken word is the symbol of a shape.

*A written word is the symbol of an* idea *as directly as a spoken word is.*

Every written word is 'paired' with a spoken word, and this spoken word means just what the written word means. In some languages, like Chinese, a written symbol is paired with more than one sound symbol. The written symbol remains the same, but the sound symbol varies from place to place. One Chinese can understand what another writes, even though he may not have any idea what the other is saying.

In a more or less phonetic language, like English, written

words happen to be composed of shapes which more or less correspond to certain sounds. And spoken words happen to be composed of sounds which more or less correspond to certain shapes.

A child *reads* a word when he sees it as a symbol, and understands what the symbol represents. He does not have to be able to say the word, or even know what it sounds like.

When we teach a child a written word in terms of its corresponding sound, we are not, strictly, teaching him to read, but to do something different—to link one kind of symbol with another. Because a child's hearing-understanding vocabulary is usually larger than his reading vocabulary, this is an efficient way of *helping* him to read.

Suppose, for example, that a baby is learning what a cup is. He drinks out of cups—'Here is your cup of milk.'—pours out of cups—'Oh, clever! You poured the water out of the cup without spilling it!'—bashes cups on top of his head—'Careful with that cup, love.'—and probably breaks cups—'Oh well. Another cup smashed.'

From these experiences, a certain order emerges. The baby forms an idea of 'cup-ness'. A cup is something that holds his milk or his juice, something to drink from, something that can tip over and spill its contents. And he can not only associate his own familiar cup with this concept which is taking shape in his mind; he can also see an *unfamiliar* cup as a new example of his concept. The strange cup may be different in colour, size and shape from any cup he has seen before, but if it has the essential qualities, *then the baby recognizes it as a cup*.

He forms the concept all by himself. No one can create it for him. But if the concept takes shape beside a *symbol*, a *word* that represents it, the baby finds it easier both to form the concept and to remember the word. The spoken sound becomes a focal point which unites the various, fleeting impressions of what a cup is, and it is remembered because it is associated with all the experiences which have built up the baby's idea of a cup.

If we now show the baby the written word 'cup', and teach him that the written shape he sees and the sound he hears *mean the same thing*, we are making all these associations available for the written word as they already are for the spoken word. It is simply a short cut — we do not have to spend time building up associations, all over again, for the written word.

Before a child has learned phonetics, we must translate the written word into sounds for him. We do this not because 'seeing the sound' is essential to reading, but because the spoken word helps to provide the meaning for the written word. Later, though, when a child has learned phonetics, he can carry out the translation by himself. This is a useful thing for him to be able to do, so it is a good idea to teach him phonetics.

Linking a written word with a spoken word is not the only way of building up its meaning, however. As our reading vocabularies grow, we learn the meanings of many written words, not by sounding them out, but by reading them in a variety of contexts. Doman concludes from this that it isn't necessary to bother with phonetics.

But it is just here that an understanding of phonetics performs a very important job — and one which has been largely ignored on both sides of the alphabet battle. If we do not know phonetics, we will understand these new written words well enough. But we won't be able to use them in our *speech* vocabularies.

The interchange of symbols works *both* ways.

A knowledge of phonetics will not only enable a child to

find out the meanings of written words by translating them into sounds; it will also enable him to pronounce new written words, made meaningful from their written context, without having to learn them as spoken words all over again. In the long run, that is an even more useful thing for him to be able to do, for he will learn many more words from his reading than from conversation. Another good reason for teaching phonetics.

It is quite true that a child does not need to know phonetics in order to understand speech. He does not need to know phonetics in order to read. But when he can hear *and* read, *then* he needs to know phonetics in order to be able to translate shape-words into sound-words, and sound-words into shape-words. Otherwise, his reading vocabulary will grow in its own terms, and his speech vocabulary will grow in *its* own terms.

An understanding of phonetics is the bridge between the two. With it, both vocabularies can grow at the same rate, and supply each other.

The nice thing about a phonetic language is that every word, whether spoken or written, carries its own pocket dictionary about with it, translating it into the other kind of symbol. When we teach a child phonetics, we are not teaching him to hear or to read, but to use that dictionary.*

Naturally, when we are helping a child of any age to understand a new language, the most efficient way of doing so is just to use that language in his presence as meaningfully as possible.

We don't *begin* with a dictionary. Or if we do, it will be a

* A written word is not the *symbol* of a sound, but the *sign* of a sound. A spoken word is, likewise, a sign of the corresponding shape. A letter does not symbolize a sound—it signifies it; and an isolated sound signifies the corresponding letter or set of letters. This distinction is useful because it helps to point up the two different mental processes involved in interpreting words. See Chapter II.

very slow business. But when he is at home with the new language, and enjoys understanding it, then we can easily show him how to use the dictionary in order to find the words he needs.

So now we are faced with another question. Tiny children may be able to understand written symbols as easily as they understand spoken symbols, and they may enjoy learning to read more than all their other play. But isn't it a bit much to suggest that we should teach them to use *dictionaries*?

Doman, I think, would say, yes, it is a bit much. The most important thing about playing the reading game—he says it again and again, because it *is* so important—is that mother and child should do it for sheer joy. If we are going to drag all the academic luggage of the classroom into the nursery, then something will go sour.

And yet I believe that we can show tiny children how to use this particular dictionary as easily as we show them how to use a spoon.

# 3

## Learning to See Sounds

My two-year-old daughter was sitting in the living-room, reading a new book of nursery rhymes to herself. I was peeling potatoes in the kitchen, listening.

'Old King Cole', declared Gwynneth, 'was a merry old sowl.'

'*Soul!*' I shouted, through the door.

'What, Mummy?'

'Not sowl. *Soul.* Old King Cole was a merry old *soul.*'

Gwynneth considered. '*No*, Mummy, that's wrong. It's got an "ow" in it.'

I put down the peeler and went over to her.

'Yes, I know, love. Just like the sound on your blackboard. Usually that sound says "ow". But sometimes it feels like a change, so it says "oh". Look, it rhymes. Old King Cole was a merry old soul. It's like saying that he was a merry old man.'

'Oh.' Gwynneth was still doubtful, but finally decided to take my word for it. As I went back to the kitchen, I heard her beginning again. 'Old King Cole was a merry old soul, And a merry old soul was he...'

I smiled, but there was a bit of a sigh in it. What she had

just done showed me that our reading game was almost over, and she was ready for take-off. Her 'mistake' meant that she really was doing what I had suspected, without being able to be sure – she was translating unfamiliar written words into sounds at a single glance.

Teaching her to read and translate words had taken eight months. She was two years and eight months old, and we had begun the reading game on her second birthday.

Is my daughter some kind of amazing prodigy? By no means. She is a perfectly normal, scatter-brained youngster, and what she has done, any average two-year-old could do. Before she had learned to read her first word, I had planned out how to teach her, spending just a few minutes a day, and had decided that it would probably take between six and eight months from start to finish. Now it was done, and like a mother bird when her offspring flaps away from the nest, I couldn't help feeling a bit sad.

Learning to 'work out' the sounds for written words phonetically seems to us a difficult task for young children because we tend to regard it as an exercise in problem-solving. We teach a child the elements of the 'code', so the argument runs, show him how to solve a few of the puzzles, and encourage him to go on from there.

This is rather like teaching a child to ride a bicycle by explaining how the pedals operate the wheels, riding it ourselves once or twice to show how it's done, and then leaving it to him.

There is another way of helping him to ride the bicycle. We can hold it steady while he mounts, and wheel it along the path for a bit. We are doing the work, but he gets the feeling of his feet going round on the pedals. After a while, we stop holding on to the handlebars and let him steer by himself. Then one day, perhaps without his even realizing it, we let go of the saddle.

True, he hasn't learned anything about problem-solving. But he can ride the bicycle.

I decided that I wasn't very interested in teaching the techniques of problem-solving, at least as far as language was concerned. What I wanted my children to be able to do was to ride the bicycle.

We began, of course, with Doman.

Doman explains that it is better if a child doesn't even know the sounds for the letters of the alphabet before he begins to read. This is because he will tend to pick out and pronounce the individual letters in a word, rather than concentrate on the symbol as a whole, and will learn more slowly than he would do otherwise. But as his reading vocabulary grows, he will probably notice the same letters recurring, and ask you what they are. Then you tell him.

I didn't bother to use the names of the letters at all, as these seemed particularly useless items of information. We used sound-names: I added an indeterminate vowel-sound to the consonants, something like the final sound in 'mother' or the vowel sound in 'bus', to make them easier to say — bu, cu, du, fu, gu, hu, ju, ku,* lu, mu, nu, pu, qu, ru, su, tu, vu, wu, ex, yu, zu. (This vowel sound, which is almost present anyway when we pronounce a final consonant emphatically, readily disappeared later on when my children were building the sounds for words.) I linked 'q' with its following 'u' from the beginning, treating the two-letter shape as a single letter. For the five vowels, we used only the short sounds to begin with. I had other plans for the long ones. Nor did I introduce the 'i' sound for 'y', the 's' sound for 'c' and the 'j' sound for 'g' until later.

* We distinguished between *short* 'cu', and *tall* 'ku'.

When I began teaching my children to read, I painted the lower half of one wall in their room with blackboard paint. This blackboard was a tremendous asset, and of course the children had a great time drawing and scribbling all over it. I would write new words on the blackboard at night, while they were asleep. By the time these words had been discovered in the morning: 'Mummy! Come and see! What do my new words say?' and I had read them, casually, at intervals during the day, and Gwynneth had read them to her dolls and other children who came by, the words had really taught themselves.

When Gwynneth had been learning to read for two months, she had read two story-books, and had a reading vocabulary of about seventy words. At this point, Doman suggests that the alphabet can be taught explicitly.

I got two alphabet books—John Burningham's *ABC*, because I fell in love with the illustrations, and the Dr Seuss *ABC*, because it is a delightfully crazy way of teaching letter sounds.

Gwynneth had picked up the sound-names for most of the letters by this time, but we spent a day on each one anyway. I put the letter and its capital on the blackboard, a word to go with it (twice, once with the capital and once with the small letter), and a picture. The old game of 'I spy' was useful at this time. We went through one of the alphabet books as far as Gwynneth had learned each day, and she often went through them of her own accord. She was learning many other words by 'look-and-understand' at the same time.

By the end of the third month, she knew all the sounds of the alphabet without hesitation.

I 'extended' the alphabet to include the following combinations, teaching them just as if they were additional letters: ai, aw, ay, ch, ck, ea, ee, er, ew, ng, oa, oo, ou, ow, ph, sh, th, wh. (The sounds for other combinations, such as 'oi', 'ur', etc., can really be worked out from the separate sounds of the two letters.) As she had not yet learned that any of these combinations had a particular sound of its own, we spent a little longer on the combinations than on the letters of the alphabet: two days for each one. I used the following words (making sure that Gwynneth could already read them as wholes) to teach the combinations: train, saw, say, chin, back, sea, tree, her, new, king, boat, room, out, cow, phone, shop, this, when.

I wrote the combination on the blackboard in red, then the 'teaching word' for that combination, with the combination in red and the rest of the word in some other colour. I also made a word card for each combination. On one side of the card I printed the combination in red. On the other side, I wrote the teaching word, again with the combination in red. When Gwynneth read one of these cards, she first pronounced the combination by itself. Then I turned over the card and she read the whole word aloud. Either I pointed out the combination in the word, or Gwynneth noticed it herself: 'Train. Oh, look – it's got an "ai" in it, Mummy!' Each day, we went through some of the combination cards she had learned so far, very quickly. Quite often I did not ask her to read them, but just read them for her myself. I also listed the combinations, without their words, at the top of the blackboard as Gwynneth learned them, and she practised saying these quite often, of her own accord – showing the kind of pleasure with which one recognizes old friends.

Just after the end of the fourth month, Gwynneth knew the sound of each combination without hesitation.

Some readers may think that we were going too fast. Doman points out that if we linger over a particular word for too long, a child will get fed up, and may read 'hippo-potamus' for 'hand'. He is not making a mistake. He is simply telling us, very politely, that he is ready to go on to something else. A small child can learn to read whole words with astonishing speed, and he learns far more easily if he goes fast than if he goes slowly. The same principle applies when we are teaching him to associate letters and sounds.

Of course, as soon as Gwynneth had learned a particular shape-sound, I pointed it out in words she already knew, and the words she was learning (still as wholes) for her story-books – or Gwynneth pointed it out to me. There was thus constant repetition, but quite naturally and meaningfully, without any need for soul-destroying drill with an isolated letter, or one word repeated over and over again. The whole process of learning to associate letters and sounds is cumula-tive, while the child's attention is mainly concentrated on the meaning of what he is reading.

When Gwynneth had learned the sounds for the alphabet and combinations, I knew that she had all the raw material she needed to be able to translate regular words indepen-dently of me. My next job was to show her how to use it. I began doing this as soon as she had finished the alphabet, at the same time as she was learning the combinations.

I should explain that Doman uses word cards to teach a child the words for his first book, and I continued to make similar cards for the first few books which Gwynneth read. I printed the word with a small letter on one side of the card, and with a capital letter on the reverse side (doll: Doll). Gwynneth knew that the word on the reverse side would be the same, but in this way she easily absorbed the way it looked with a capital letter.

Now I put this knowledge to further use. On one side of a card, I printed a two-letter word Gwynneth could already read: 'in'. On the reverse side, I printed the two letters separately: 'i  n'. I showed Gwynneth this side of the card first, and she translated the letters separately. I turned over the card, and she read aloud the whole word. Without my saying anything, I was showing her that the two sounds 'i' and 'n' were the 'same' as the whole word 'in'.

Then I made this more explicit. I wrote the word 'in' on the blackboard. Gwynneth read it aloud. We played hide-and-seek. I covered up the 'n' and Gwynneth said: 'ĭ'. I covered up the 'i' and Gwynneth said: 'nu'. I uncovered the word, and Gwynneth read it as a whole once again. '*That's* right!' I said. ' "ĭ" and "nu" make "in", don't they? Clever girl! You *are* doing well!'

In the same way, we analysed am, an, as, at, if, is, it, of, on, up, us: all words which Gwynneth could already read. We spent a day on each one, and went through both sides of some of the word cards every now and then. Again, I often translated these letters and words for her, instead of asking her to do so.

You will notice that this still had nothing to do with problem-solving. I was not asking Gwynneth to translate anything which she had not already learned. It was still, in fact, '*look-and-say*'. We teach a child *phonetics* by 'look-and-say'! We teach him to *read* by 'look-and-understand'.

Two-letter words are quite easy to translate into sounds. So are three-letter words. It is when we move on to longer words, like 'whisker', or 'fresh', that things begin to get complicated. Before I describe how we tackled three-letter words, I would like to show you how we tackled the longer words, so that you can see what I was aiming at.

Here is a child in school trying to work out the sound for the unfamiliar written word 'basket'. *Child* (making the sounds): 'b, a, s, k, e, t.' *Teacher:* 'That's right! So what does

the word say?' Child looks blank. *Teacher:* 'Well, go through
the sounds again, a bit more quickly.' *Child* (getting bored):
'b, a, s, k, e, t'. *Teacher:* 'Well?' *Child:* 'Er—' *Teacher*
(coming to the rescue): 'Well, it says "basket", doesn't it—
b, a, s, k, e, t—basket.' *Child:* 'Oh.' (Thinks wistfully of bag
of marbles in his pocket.)

Here is my two-year-old daughter tackling the same
word: I cover up all but the 'b'. Gwynneth says: 'bu'. I uncover the next letter. Gwynneth says: 'ba'. I uncover the
next one. Gwynneth says: 'bas'. The next one. Gwynneth
says: 'bask'. The next one. Gwynneth says: 'baske'. Last
one. Gwynneth says: 'basket. Oh!' (Sudden realization);
'Basket!'

Job done.

This is a very simple refinement of a basically conventional way of teaching phonetics. But it is, I think, a refinement which makes all the difference. It makes the job
manageable. A child doesn't get lost in the middle of the
word. He adds one bit at a time—and quite often guesses the
sound for the whole word when he is only halfway through.

We called it the 'building game'.

I didn't expect Gwynneth to be able to play this game by
herself before I had played it with her many times, and I
used three-letter words to show her how to play.

We began with the word 'bad', which Gwynneth could
already read. I made a word card for it. On one side of the
card I printed the whole word by itself. On the reverse side,
I printed 'b ba bad'. I taught Gwynneth these three shape-
sounds by 'look-and-say', and she learned them very
quickly. We made it into a kind of chanting game.

I turned the card over, and Gwynneth read the complete
word. Then we played hide-and-seek with it. I covered up
all but the 'b'. Gwynneth said: 'bu'. I uncovered the 'a';

4

Gwynneth said: 'ba'. I uncovered the 'd' and once again Gwynneth said the complete word.

You will notice again that I was not asking Gwynneth to say anything which she had not already learned.

In the same way, we played hide-and-seek with 30 three-part words: bad, can, has, jam, man, sat; bed, fell, get, let, red, yes; big, did, him, his, pig, sit; box, dog, doll, got, hot, top; bus, but, cup, fun, run, sun. These are all, by the way, Key Words*—common words which occur with great frequency in children's books—and Gwynneth could read most of them already. We played the game with two new words a day, and went over some of the word cards Gwynneth already knew at intervals.

Two and a half months after we began the alphabet, Gwynneth knew the sounds for the alphabet and the combinations, and could analyse 12 two-letter words and 30 three-letter words. She hadn't solved any problems, and I was still wheeling the bicycle.

Now when I taught Gwynneth new regular words for her story-books, I covered them first and built them up, letter-sound by letter-sound, sometimes encouraging Gwynneth to repeat these sounds after me. (When we met a combination, I uncovered the two letters at once.) After a while, Gwynneth was able to play the building game with any word which I had already built for her a few times, while I uncovered the letters.

Then she was able to play the game with other words which she could already read, but which I had not built up for her—words like 'mop', 'then', 'much'.

And then, almost without her realizing it, the habit began to spread to words which she could not already read. Three

* See the Ladybird Key Words Reading Scheme which I hope will be extended to simple story-books as soon as possible.

and a half months after we had begun the alphabet, Gwynneth could play the building game with new words like 'tail', 'indeed', 'gave' and 'proud'. I was still giving her a lot of help, uncovering the letters myself and making it as difficult as possible for her to make a mistake. Here, for example, is how we tackled a word like 'proud' at this point:

I cover all but the 'p'. *Gwynneth*: 'pu.' I uncover 'pr'. *Gwynneth*: 'pr.' I cover the beginning and end of the word so only the 'ou' is visible. *Mum*: 'Look — that's like one of the sounds on your blackboard.' *Gwynneth*: 'Oh yes! Ou!' *Mum* (uncovering 'prou'): 'So now it says pr — ?' *Gwynneth*: 'prou.' *Mum* (excited): 'Very good! — now what's this little letter?' (pointing to the 'd'). *Gwynneth*: 'du.' *Mum*: 'That's right! So now the word says prou — ?' *Gwynneth*: 'proud!' *Mum*: 'Oh! Clever!' (Hugs and exclamations.)

I had let go of the handlebars, and Gwynneth was steering by herself.

Let me bring out something interesting at this point. Gwynneth had translated the word 'proud' into sounds. *But she hadn't read it.*

The word came up in the Ladybird edition of *The Gingerbread Boy* (the series with the irresistible illustrations), which Gwynneth was reading at the time, in the sentence: 'He began to feel very proud of his running.' After we had built up the sound of the word, Gwynneth said: 'What does "proud" mean, Mummy?'

'Well, it means he was very, very pleased with himself — the way you felt when you jumped off the step for the first time.'

Gwynneth looked at the word 'proud' again, and this time she saw it as something completely different — a transparent whole, a symbol. And behind the symbol, a single thread of meaning. The next time she read *The Gingerbread Boy*—and she did, on her own, often—she would see the word 'proud' in the same way. As she read it in different books and in different contexts, she would go on seeing it in the same way, and the web of meaning behind the symbol would grow.

And if she wanted to, she would be able to translate that symbol into sounds.

This is what I mean by saying that reading is something totally different from happening to know the sounds for the words that we read, and that when we teach a child phonetics, we are *not* teaching him to read. Our confusion over reading has come about because our associations are so strong that we usually see a word as a symbol and as a sound simultaneously—and poets use our 'double vision' to give poetry its peculiar force. But we cannot read a word when we see it as a sound. We can read it only when we see it as a symbol.

We need not be afraid of letting children come across written symbols that they cannot understand—or of letting them translate those symbols into sounds. As they see the symbols, in a meaningful context, they will learn to understand them—it is just as easy for a child to learn a new word through his eyes as through his ears.

How did we tackle the long vowel sound in words like 'gave', 'time', 'tune' and 'poke'? We played the building game with those words just as we did with others, saying 'su, sa, sam'—and then a magic 'ĕ' hopped out and changed the 'ă' into an 'ā', making the word say 'same'. Gwynneth was very impressed with the 'e's cleverness! I played the game for her many times with words like these which were cropping up in her story-books, and she gradually acquired the habit of doing it herself. The long vowel sounds were thus taught quite incidentally, as we played with the words. I didn't explain that the 'e' was a silent letter; I just showed Gwynneth how it worked. By the time she was building these words by herself, she understood perfectly that the 'e' was not pronounced.

Sometimes, naturally, she gave a big wobble, and then I just steadied the bike a bit. If she was going through a long word like 'teacher', she sometimes muddled it, going 't, tea, touch...' I didn't make her go through it again from the beginning. I prompted her by repeating the word as far as she had said it correctly, and then waited for her to add the next sound. If she still couldn't manage it, I added it for her. *I didn't want to make a task of it.* I just wanted her to 'see' the sound arrangement correctly.

Seven months after Gwynneth began learning to read, she could play the building game with new words like 'rooster', 'fresh', 'shutters' and 'whisker'. She had a reading vocabulary of about 1,000 words, and could read anything that she could understand.

In a little while she needed no prompting when she was building the sounds for many words, and she was uncovering the letters by herself. Mum, hands off the saddle at last, stood and watched her go. But Gwynneth scarcely realized that I was no longer there.

The building game itself is just a crutch, and the final stage is reached when it is no longer necessary. When Gwynneth read 'Old King Cole' as I described at the beginning of the chapter, I realized that for simple words, at least, this stage had been reached. She had seen the sound for the whole word 'soul' in one glance. She wasn't thinking about the pedals any more, or how to turn the handlebars.

In fact, she wasn't thinking about the bicycle at all. She was thinking about where she was going.

You may imagine that we spent long hours every day on all this, but we didn't. I reckoned to spend about twenty minutes a day on actual teaching — ten minutes in the morning, ten minutes in the afternoon — and this included the time Gwynneth spent reading her story-books to me. Sometimes it took a bit longer — if she was determined to go all the way through one of her books, and ordered me to stop and listen until she had finished. Of course, there were other times when I read stories to her. And she could pick up her books and go through them any time she pleased, which she often did.

I never made Gwynneth play the reading game. If she hadn't felt like playing, we wouldn't have played — but I can't remember that this ever happened.

All this time, I went on teaching her the sounds for irregular words without building them up, but at this point she could guess the sound symbols for words which had only slight irregularities, if these words were already part of her hearing vocabulary.

Some educationists and teachers feel that irregular words are a great obstacle to a beginning reader, and the initial teaching alphabet (the i.t.a. — a much more regular phonetic translation of speech) is one medium which has been developed to avoid the problem. A growing amount of evidence suggests that the i.t.a. does in fact make reading easier for children.

But the i.t.a. cannot, in itself, affect the speed with which a child learns to associate a written word with its meaning, for that depends on the number of times he pays attention to the word and its meaning together. The i.t.a. really achieves only one thing. It enables a child to translate into sounds, by himself, unfamiliar written words which are ordinarily spelled in an irregular way. As a result, if he knows the meaning of the spoken word, he can find out the meaning of the written word by himself. This means that he can teach *himself* to read some 'difficult' written words, instead of depending on outside help.

So it seems that we must conclude that the i.t.a. makes reading lessons easier for the *teacher*, but not necessarily for the *child*. For we can help the child to see the meaning every bit as quickly by just telling him the sound symbols for the irregular words he meets, whenever he asks, however often he asks. And surely that is what parents and teachers are there *for*. Learning to *read* these words happens as the child goes on meeting them in context, and as he goes on seeing and understanding them, he has no difficulty in associating them with the equivalent spoken words.

The big disadvantage of the i.t.a. is that the written words which naturally surround a small child—on cereal packets, billboards, television and so on—are spelled in the ordinary way; the choice of reading material in i.t.a. is severely limited, and if a child learns to read as fast as he *can* learn, he will have to switch to ordinary spelling within a matter of months.

An adult can understand the English written language, with all its anomalies, all its idiosyncracies, all its throughs, boughs, coughs, doughs and enoughs. So can a child. We don't need a whole battery of sophisticated media. All we need is a child, and a certain amount of insight into how he learns. Glenn Doman has given us this insight.

# 4

## Helping Your Child to Read

Gwynneth learned phonetics very quickly because she learned to read very quickly, and learning phonetics was simply a matter of playing games with the words she was reading. Almost all tiny children are capable of learning to read as quickly as they learn to understand speech, and we are far more likely to bore them by going too slowly than by going too fast.

In this chapter, I would like to fill in some more details about aids and approaches to the teaching of reading and phonetics which you might find useful. My elder daughter, Helen, learned to read at three and a quarter, and I describe her development mainly, to avoid jumping from one to the other, but indicate if Gwynneth responded differently.

### I. A blackboard in the children's room

The idea of a blackboard occurred to me because even at three and a quarter Helen was an independent creature, anxious to be off about her own concerns, and apt to get a bit impatient with Mum's cards. I thought another approach might be helpful. As our walls were painted cement, we simply painted the bottom half of one wall in the children's room with blackboard paint.

You may well find that it is worth a little trouble to provide your own children with a 'toy' like this. If you have a wall that can be painted, you can always paint over the blackboard paint when the blackboard is no longer needed. Otherwise, a big piece of hardboard, similarly painted, will do just as well. If a blackboard gives you unpleasant memories of school and formal education, remember that it has no associations for pre-school toddlers but is a marvellous place for messing about with chalk!

If you are seriously interested in helping your children to read and write, a blackboard will be so useful that it would be a pity to try and manage without one.

Words written stealthily on the blackboard at night, ready to be discovered in the morning, practically teach themselves by the end of the following day. When Helen woke up, she was the one who came to me, demanding to know what the words said. I left about half a dozen 'old' words on the blackboard at any one time, and I would rearrange these so that I knew Helen was really reading them, and not just remembering their positions. I had word cards as well, and now she enjoyed matching these with their counterparts on the blackboard.

The blackboard was also very helpful when I wanted to show Helen how to follow the order of written words. This is a problem which often vexes educationists. How do we teach a child where to begin? James Thompson, in *Educating Your Baby*, says that: 'in order to read and write, the child requires a sense of left and right. A child frequently starts at the right and proceeds to the left, or even starts in the middle.' Dr Engelmann, in *Give Your Child A Superior Mind*, suggests a way of tackling the 'problem': 'The parent should get the child to locate all the words in a piece, going from left to right. Get him to touch every word. (He may not have the motor ability to touch every word he wants to touch, but on no account rush him.)'

This is the exact opposite of the approach we use when a child is learning to understand speech. Luckily it hasn't yet occurred to us to present a baby with a jumble of spoken words, and ask him to locate the one he thinks he ought to understand first. Because speech uses a time sequence, rather than a space sequence, we have very fortunately arranged spoken language so that it automatically reaches a baby's ears in a meaningful order.

We can do the same thing when he is learning to read. If he doesn't know how to locate the words himself, then we must locate them for him. When Helen was beginning to read sentences, I would leave a sentence on the blackboard throughout the day, and read it to her at intervals, pointing to each word as I read it. (I did this even though I always used words she could already read.) When she was beginning to read books, I pointed to the word I wanted her to read next. She was very soon pointing by herself, and as her reading speeded up, she stopped pointing altogether.

It isn't necessary to waste time teaching a child the difference between left and right before we begin helping him to understand written language. It isn't necessary to teach him how to follow the stories in strip cartoons and comic books in order to accustom him to the conventional direction of written words.

It is much simpler just to show him the way a sentence goes.

Later, when we began phonetics, the blackboard helped Helen to learn the sounds for the alphabet and the letter combinations. And I found, to my surprise, that both children were tracing over the outlines of the letters on the blackboard, and trying to copy them. Although I ignored this for quite a long time, I gradually realized that children who could already read, and enjoyed reading, also wanted to learn to write.

## II. Ways of using word cards

Doman implies that once your child has learned all the words in the Doman kit, and read his first book, he will go forward on his own, asking for your help when he meets an unfamiliar word. This may not be so, however, and you may feel, as I did, that your child needs to learn individual words, before meeting them in a book he is reading, for quite a while longer. This helps him to read a new book more rapidly and confidently, and when he does not have to stop and ask for your help at every tenth word he learns sooner how enjoyable reading is.

*Listing words*

So when Helen was going to begin reading a new book, I would go through it first, listing all the new words. I found it helpful to enter these new words in a master list, arranged under letters of the alphabet, of all the words she had learned, so that I could easily check to see whether she had learned a particular word or not. (This may seem rather troublesome, but it isn't necessary for more than the first few books.) I also discovered that it was useful to put the initials of the book title (or some identification) beside each word in this alphabetical list. Then if we did not use a book after all, I would know which words to cross out. I found it interesting to look through this list, and see how Helen's vocabulary was growing.

*Identifying the cards*

I made a word card for each of these new words. (Again

it is useful to identify these cards with the initials of the book title, especially if you plan to use the cards for more than one child. Let your children play with the box of word cards in one weak moment on a rainy afternoon, as I did, and re-sorting unidentified cards will be a major headache.) As our work with phonetics progressed, I did not make cards for more and more of the simpler words. Helen translated these herself as she met them in her books.

## Teaching variations in words

These word cards give you an ideal way of teaching different forms of the same word. As soon as Helen was reading books, I printed the same word beginning with a capital letter on the back of the card (here: Here). Some children's books use simplified forms of some letters (a, g and y, for example), and when we wanted to read these I printed the word with simplified letters on the reverse side of the card (gray: gray). Plurals were introduced in a similar way almost from the beginning (bed: Beds) – and gradually, as Helen's vocabulary grew, more and more variations: the 'ed' and 'ing' forms of a verb (laugh: laughed; run: running); and still later, the reverse sides helped her to build up different words (grand: grand-mother; night: goodnight). Helen knew that the pairs were always related in some way, and this helped her to learn the longer words.

## Size of cards

I began by making these word cards very big (see Doman's book), but once the beginning stages were over, I found that even my two-year-old could read words printed on cards roughly 6 inches by $2\frac{1}{2}$ inches. Large sheets of card 25 inches by 20 inches cut up into 32 of these. Or you may be able to

buy packets of blank cards. Card is better than paper because it is tougher, and also lettering done with felt-tipped
marking pens shows through even stiff paper. I made
lower-case 'a's and 'c's, etc., about $\frac{3}{4}$ inch high.

The same words were first written on the blackboard in
much larger letters, and the word cards helped my daughters
to make the transition to book print.

*Using the cards: reading sessions*

We soon developed a routine which proved popular enough
to keep to fairly well, though I let it slip every now and
then when we seemed to be getting stale. Once it had become a habit, though, it was Helen who complained if we
left anything out. You may find something like this works
for you; or you may find it easier to spread the sessions in
more little bits through the day; or you may find that just
before bed-time is the only possible time, if your days are
very busy.

Early in the morning the new words would be discovered
on the blackboard, and quite often I would be dragged out
of bed to reveal what they said. At first I read the words
aloud straight away. When Helen had learned the sounds
for the letters, I encouraged her to build up the sounds for
each word, and see if she could translate the words by
herself. If she couldn't, I did not insist, but translated them
for her, usually pointing out how the sounds fitted the
letters.

Later on, morning elevenses would be followed by
'reading time'. Words on cards would be matched with
words on the blackboard; Helen or I would sound them out
again; we would look at the backs of the cards; and Helen
would read five or ten cards (some old ones and the new
ones). Quite often I did not test Helen at all as we went

through the cards. I read one side, and turned it over for her to read the same word on the reverse side.

Then Helen would read me a page or so from her current book. She would read a new book as she learned the words for it, and usually she would read until she met the words she hadn't learned. I would encourage her to try working out the sounds for two or three of these on her own, telling her what they said if she couldn't manage it; then we would stop the session. After that, it was Mum's turn to read a story.

My husband helped by asking to be shown the blackboard when he came home: he was led importantly to the children's room and given a reading lesson!

We had 'reading time' again just before bed-time.

This routine worked particularly well with Helen. If I waited for odd times when I had a few minutes to spare she would probably be engrossed in her own games, and resent interruption. With Gwynneth I was more flexible, as she was generally eager to drop everything and play the reading game whenever I suggested it. (It seems to me that it is partly because a two-year-old is so distractible that he is easier to teach. Whatever he was absorbed in even two minutes before is forgotten, and he concentrates his entire small self on the words his mother shows him. A child of school age goes on thinking about the castle he was building, and the teacher has to work that much harder to engage his total attention.)

I found that it helped, when testing Gwynneth in the early stages, to follow Doman's suggestion of saying: 'Where is the word that says—?' instead of: 'What does this say?' even though she was talking quite well when I began teaching her. Also, I tested her only at night for a long time, and told her what the words said when I showed them to her during the day, even if she already knew them.

At first, Helen learned new words at the rate of one word a day. A month later, she was learning two words a day, and two months after that, between six and ten words every day with no trouble at all.

Many people find it difficult to believe that a child can learn to understand and distinguish between hundreds of written words with little help from phonetic translation. But although we had made a beginning with phonetics by this time (i.e. four months after Helen began learning to read) she could not yet translate most of her new written words into sounds by herself. Her rapidly increasing rate of learning new words clearly sprang from her growing power to associate written words with their meanings.

Once we have understood that interpreting written language is *exactly* comparable to interpreting speech, we can see how all the apparent difficulties which face a small child who is reading for the first time simply disappear. And so they should, for they are nothing more than so many paper tigers. As I have tried to show, the key is to ask ourselves: 'How is this difficulty overcome when a child is understanding speech?' and the way of dealing with the problem becomes clear.

For example, much has been written about the similarity between 'b' and 'd', 'p' and 'q', and so on, and the necessity for teaching a child the difference between right and left so that he can distinguish between these letters. We have not stopped to think that the *sound* 'b' is very similar to the *sound* 'p'; the *sound* 'd' to the *sound* 't'; the *sound* 'm' to the *sound* 'n', and so on. And yet a small child has no difficulty in understanding spoken words which contain these sounds. Why not?

The difference lies in the way he learns the words. To begin with, we are not constantly testing him to see if he has understood what we have said. We just talk to him, trying to put things as clearly as possible in terms of his own experience. If he shows by what he says that he has misunderstood, we explain more clearly still. We use the word in a *context* which is designed to supply the meaning of the word that has been misunderstood.

We *don't* make him repeat 'p' and 'b' twenty times a day.

We *don't* say: 'No, I didn't say "pig". Listen again. Bu, i, gu. Now, what word did I say?'

We say: 'No, not "pig", darling — "big". A great bi-i-ig giant — oh, taller than the house!' And he understands us perfectly.

When he is learning to read, we can use the same kind of approach. Suppose he is reading a word card, and says 'dig' instead of 'big'. Then we *don't* tell him he is wrong and ask him to try again. We simply correct him. 'No, not "dig" — "big".' If we want to, we can point out the 'b' and remind him that it looks different from 'd'. (It isn't necessary at this point to stress that 'b' has a different *sound* from 'd', for the difference in appearance is more important than the difference in the corresponding sounds.) But the main thing is to make sure that the child reads 'big' in a meaningful context as soon as possible. When he has read and understood it in his story-books a few times, he will have no difficulty with it at all.

## Phonic words

You will need special word cards as you begin to teach your child phonetics. (In a very short time, you will simply use the words he is meeting in his story-books.) Here are what **you** will need:

*Two-letter words*: 12 cards: am, an, as, at, if, in, is, it, of, on, up, us.

On one side of the card, print the word 'am'. (There is no need to use simplified letters. Your child is probably more used to reading the others. The letters should be the same size as for his other word cards – i.e. 'a's and 'c's ¾ inch high.) On the other side of the same card, print the same two letters separately: 'a m'. Make similar cards for each of the other two-letter words listed.

*Three-letter words* (these cards will need to be quite a bit longer than the cards for two-letter words): 30 cards: bad, can, has, jam, man, sat; bed, fell, get, let, red, yes; big, did, him, his, pig, sit; box, dog, doll, got, not, top; bus, but, cup, fun, run, sun. (Four-letter words such as 'fell' and 'doll' are easily treated like three-letter words.)

On one side of one card, print 'bad'. On the other side of the same card, print 'b ba bad'. Make similar cards for each of the other three-letter words listed. (Print 'f fe fell', 'd do doll'.)

*Letter combinations*: 18 cards. Print the combination (ai) on one side of the card in red, or some other bright colour. On the other side of the same card, print the word you are using to teach that combination. Use red for the combination, and black for the rest of the word (**tra**in).

Here are the combinations and words: **ai**, tr**ai**n; **aw**, s**aw**; **ay**, s**ay**; **ch**, **ch**in; **ck**, ba**ck**; **ea**, s**ea**; **ee**, tr**ee**; **er**, h**er**; **ew**, n**ew**; **ng**, ki**ng**; **oa**, b**oa**t; **oo**, r**oo**m; **ou**, **ou**t; **ow**, c**ow**; **ph**, **ph**one; **sh**, **sh**op; **th**, **th**is; **wh**, **wh**en.

Some of the combinations do not always make the given sound. I have used the sounds they most commonly make. When they made 'irregular' sounds, I taught the sounds for those words without building them up. I have not given the alternative short sound for 'oo' (as in 'book') – when this

5

sound occurs, it can really be guessed from the long 'oo' sound given. The same is true of the unvoiced 'th' sound (as in 'think', 'throw'). The sounds for 'oi' (as in 'voice'), 'oy' (as in 'toy'), 'ar' (as in 'car'), 'ur' (as in 'nurse') and 'ir' (as in 'first') can be built up from the separate sounds of the two letters. I felt that the alternative sound for 'ow' (as in 'elbow') would be confusing, and taught the sounds for such words without building them up. There are one or two other combinations (e.g. 'ui' in 'juice'), but these don't occur very often, and there is little point in teaching the individual sounds for them. Remember you don't want to give your child an academic knowledge of the sound for every variation—just the tools he will need to translate most new words.

### III. A note on story time

Reading stories to your children is worth most as an end in itself, and it would be a great pity to stop reading to him just because he can read himself. In addition to sheer enjoyment, which is the best reason for doing it, you can go on opening up new worlds and interests for your children right through the junior school years in this simple way. We can take more of a hand in our children's education than we are apt to think.

Reading to him is also one of the best ways of increasing your child's own reading ability. It is another of the reasons (quite apart from age this time) why you, as his mother, can teach your own child to read more effectively than his teacher can: simply because you can hold the book so that your child can see the print while you read. (Teachers can find ways of doing the same thing, but it is more difficult with forty children than with one or two.) Once Helen was reading easily, I found that she could read almost any book which I had read to her several times. She was reading each word, not reciting by heart; she had learned the unfamiliar words as I read. She could also recognize these words in other contexts. I had never *asked* her to follow the print, although I sometimes pointed out new words as we went along.

Doman indicates that children widen their reading vocabularies by being read to, but I think that the point bears emphasizing, particularly for the later stages. It follows from Doman's theory that any child, of any age, is potentially capable of reading any book which he can understand when it is read to him. In other words, provided he is given enough initial help, there need be no gap between what he can understand and what he can read.

(The effect of this gap is interesting. If your child begins reading early enough, the gap will be very small to begin with, and this is the ideal. A three- or four-year-old child's enjoyment increases visibly when the gap is closed. The gap for a non-reading five-year-old, particularly one brought up on television, can be very large — this is why he often finds reading boring and frustrating when he makes a beginning at school.)

Reading to your child works the other way round as well! You can help him to *understand* a new book, and so be able to read it himself, by reading it to him first. For if he begins learning to read when he is very young, he may reach the point when he can learn new words faster than he can cope with more complicated stories. If this happens, do not feel that he must always tackle a new book from scratch. Reading it to him first, with enjoyment and expression, will help him to follow the story, and also help him to read it with more fluency and expression himself. (He will have read several books by this time, and you will know that he is really reading each word, rather than just remembering the spoken words. You can always check with word cards.)

For example, Gwynneth began reading *The King, The Mice and The Cheese* when she was two years and five months. She learned the new words easily, but got rather bogged down as we went through the book. I realized that she was losing track of the story as she went along, but I also felt that the book was within her understanding if she was helped.

So we dropped her reading for a few days, and I read the book to her once or twice, in a squeaky-mouse voice, a growly-lion voice, a worried-king voice, and so on. We lingered over the illustrations and talked about them too. Gwynneth loved it, and a day or so later read the whole book through at a sitting, refusing to stop when I suggested it, and ordering me to sit and listen until she had finished. She was reading more fluently, and having a good try at the growly lion and the squeaky mouse!

It is a good idea to re-read to your child story-books that he can already read himself, putting a lot of excitement and fun into the story as you read. This will encourage him to go through these books again, on his own.

## IV. Notes on the building game

When your child has learned the alphabet, use the phonic word cards and the blackboard to show him how the sounds for two-letter words and three-letter words are built up, as I have described in Chapter 3. Teach him the combinations at the same time.

### A sound chart

When you have worked through the 30 three-letter words, you may find it helpful to write up the following chart on

| a | e | i | o | u |
|---|---|---|---|---|
| ba | be | bi | bo | bu |
| ca | — | — | co | cu |
| da | de | di | do | du |
| fa | fe | fi | fo | fu |
| ga | ge | gi | go | gu |
| ha | he | hi | ho | hu |
| ja | je | ji | jo | ju |
| ka | ke | ki | — | — |
| la | le | li | lo | lu |
| ma | me | mi | mo | mu |
| na | ne | ni | no | nu |
| pa | pe | pi | po | pu |
| qua | que | qui | — | — |
| ra | re | ri | ro | ru |
| sa | se | si | so | su |
| ta | te | ti | to | tu |
| va | ve | vi | vo | vu |
| — | we | wi | — | — |

the blackboard, one line a day to begin with. Teach the sound for each two-letter shape by 'look-and-say'. Your child may be able to translate some of the shapes by himself. He will enjoy chanting these 'nonsense' syllables, and it will be quite easy to make a game of it. Remember how he relished sounds for their own sake when he was learning to talk—he will find the same pleasure in these, unless you try very hard to convince him that they're dull! When he has learned them, he will be able to make a flying start with the sounds for most new words.

If you don't have a blackboard, he will learn the same material, if more slowly, as you go on playing the building game with him.

Some of these shapes your child knows already, as two-letter words with a different sound—be, do, go, he, me, no, so, to, we. (As a matter of interest, the rule here is that a final vowel is long, but don't bother him with that.) Just explain to him that: 'Sometimes it says "hee", sometimes it says "hĕ",' and he will accept this quite readily.

## Double consonants

Double consonants (as in 'ra**bb**it') need give you no trouble. You can uncover one letter at a time ('rab', 'rabb') and make the same sound twice. I chose several words with double consonants while I was playing the building game with Helen, and she soon got the idea.

## 'Double' words

Many longer words are made up of short bits ('gar-den', 'rab-bit', 'hid-den', tar-get', etc.). Some teachers teach the sound for each part separately; then the child is supposed to put them together. But Helen found it easier to go straight through such words. Building words right through from the beginning is really less complicated. And a child has only one meaning to think about—not a confusion of meanings ('car' and 'rot') to make into a *new* meaning ('carrot').

Words like 'something' and 'everywhere' are genuine double words, and your child will be able to read them when he knows each part separately. Cover up half of these words to help him, if necessary.

*The magic 'ĕ'*

Your child will not find it difficult to understand the magic 'ĕ' if you show him often enough how it works. Later, he will probably need a helpful question: 'Well, what does the "ĕ" do to the "ā" — or the "ī"?' Later still, the process will become automatic.

Here are some more words with a magic 'ĕ'. As far as possible, play the building game with them as they come up in your child's reading:

**a**
bake, cake, came, game, gave, grape, lake, late, made, make, name, plate, safe, shake, skate, taste.

**i**
dive, fire, five, hide, kite, like, nine, pie, prize, ride, shine, slide, smile, tie, time, tired, wipe.

**o**
alone, clothes, home, joke, poke, phone, pole, rode, rope, rose, toe, smoke, woke.

**u**
parachute, true, tube, Tuesday, tune, use.

Your child needs to know the rule about the magic 'ĕ' to be able to translate these words by himself.

There are very few words where an 'e' following a consonant lengthens an earlier 'e' ('scene' is one); the long 'e' sound is usually represented by 'ee' or 'ea'. 'U' is sometimes lengthened to 'you' ('tube') and sometimes to 'oo' ('blue'). If you think this will be confusing, just teach the sounds for 'u' words without building them up, as there are not very many such words, and explain the 'u' rule later on.

An 'e' which follows a 'c' or 'g' usually softens these consonants to 's' and 'j'. Here are some examples:

**c**

ceiling, cent, lace, face, fence, grace, mice, nice, trace.

**g**

age, budge, bridge, danger, fudge, large, page, nudge, rage, sludge, wage.

You can point out to your child how the magic 'ĕ' works in these words, but so long as he has a basic knowledge of shape-sounds, he does not *have* to know the rule to be able to translate the words by himself. This is because the 'e' is always next to the consonant, and he will gradually learn to see 'ce' and 'ge' as single sounds – rather like combinations. For example, if he has learned the sounds for 'budge', 'bridge' and 'fudge' as wholes, he will probably be able to see the sounds for 'nudge' and 'sludge' by himself, even without being able to tell you what the 'e' does to the 'g'. I taught these words to Helen by 'look-and-understand', going on to point out the effect of the 'e', and sometimes building up the sounds of the words ('c, ca, cag, cage'; 'r, ra, rak, race') – then I left the rest to her.

'I' after 'c' and 'g' has the same effect ('city', 'giant'). As these words were comparatively few in the early stages, I simply taught their sounds without building them up for quite a long while. Later on, I showed Helen what the 'i' was doing. Here are some others:

**c**

accident, circle, icicle, magician, scissors.

**g**

giraffe, magic, magician.

'Y' does the same thing ('cycle', 'gym') but happens even less often, and I didn't explain it.

All this may seem rather complicated to you, but explain

it gradually and simply as examples crop up, and you will be surprised to find even a tiny child understanding how one letter can change the sound of another. He understands about magicians and spells: the magic 'ĕ' can be part of the same enchanted world.

## Combinations

When your child is uncovering the letters by himself, he may have a slight problem with combinations, as he will not know when to uncover two letters or one. When this happens, uncover the word for him, and let him do the rest. Remind him to look out for combinations, and it won't be very long before he has no trouble with them. (Call the combinations 'sounds' as opposed to single 'letters' if you want a simple term to use with your child—not exact, but useful.) It may help him if you write new words with combinations on the blackboard, using red for the combination, and reminding him to uncover two letters when the colour is red.

## Plastic letters

A set of plastic letters is excellent for playing the building game. Choose a set with plenty of lower-case letters, not just capitals. Helen would pick out one of her word cards (I would take care to see that the word was regular) and I helped her to find the letters, Helen following the word on the card to find out which letter was needed next. As each letter went into place, Helen added on the corresponding sound, and told me what the new shape said.

## V. How much time will it take?

Here is an approximate time-scheme for teaching your child phonetics.

He has already read at least one book, and has a reading vocabulary of 70 to 100 words or more.

*One month*: the alphabet

*The next month and a half*: ⎫ the combinations
⎬ two-letter words; three-
⎭ letter words

*The next month*: ⎫ sound chart
⎭ longer words

*The following months*: go on playing the building game

This may seem fast, and you should not keep to this rate if your child gets bored or fed up; but as Doman points out, he is much more apt to get bored if you go too slowly for him. (Of course it would be quite wrong to pressure your child to keep to this time-scheme, or any other – simply be ready to go as fast as you realize he can go.)

If you are teaching a one-year-old to read, you can teach him phonetics as soon as you reach the alphabet, exactly as I taught Gwynneth. It may take him longer to be able to play the building game himself, but you can go on playing it for him, encouraging him to repeat the sound after you as you uncover each letter. Play the game with the longer words he learns to read, as well as with the short ones.

# 5

## Step by Step with a Two-year-old

Here is the diary of my two-year-old's progress which I kept while she was learning to read.

The books listed* are not, of course, the only ones that can be used; simply available ones that I liked. They should give some indication of the kind of reading material that a two-year-old can understand.

The 'Doman books' (*Who Are You?*, *Nose is not Toes* and *Who Am I?*) may seem slightly odd to many adults, and in fact I did not use them straight away with Gwynneth. But when we started on *Who Are You?* she entered into it with great enjoyment, and I realized that the book had hidden strengths: its use of rhyme, and its use of words for parts of the body and objects around the house (e.g. nose, ear, knee, door, sink, floor). Gwynneth responded to these by gleefully banging the various bits of herself, and rushing all over the house to wallop doors, sinks, floors and so on, even before reading the words aloud. If I could have obtained the other two books, I would have used them as well at this point. The books may be less effective with children of school age.

*April 21st, 1967.* Gwynneth's second birthday. I began

* For full details see Bibliography, p. 163.

teaching her to read. She already knew two or three words and some letters from my work with Helen.

*April 25th.* Knew difference between 'mummy' and 'daddy'.

*April 26th.* Began the Doman 'self' vocabulary. Learning one word a day.

*May 17th.* Gwynneth knew the 'self' vocabulary. Began vocabulary for 'Miss P' (a homemade book about her doll): 16 new words.

*May 19th.* After Gwynneth had learned the words for the first sentence, I wrote the sentence on the blackboard, reading it to her several times a day. Then she read the same sentence in smaller print on one page of her new book.

*June 4th.* Finished learning the words for 'Miss P'. Gwynneth learned each sentence in the same way as the first one. Each time she learned a sentence, a new page was added to her book, and she read all the pages she had learned so far. (This is how a child learns to read the first book in the Doman kit. Gwynneth did not read the Doman book until later.)

*June 6th.* Gwynneth began learning words for *Puppies and Kittens*: 46 new words. Learning two words a day. I continued writing the sentences on the blackboard and reading them to her. I pointed at each word for her as she read through the book.

*June 30th.* Gwynneth began learning the alphabet while she was learning the last few words for *Puppies and Kittens*. Learning three words a day (two book words, one alphabet word).

*July 6th.* Finished reading *Puppies and Kittens*. Began vocabulary for first book in the Doman kit — *Who Are You?*: 37 new words. Gwynneth was now following the order of the words, pointing to each one by herself, without my

STEP BY STEP WITH A TWO-YEAR-OLD

help. A new page was added to the loose-leaf book as soon as she had learned the words for it, as for 'Miss P'.

*July 19th.* Began working with two-letter words, as Gwynneth had learned all the necessary letters. Put 'i', 'f', 'n', 's' and 't' on the blackboard until she was completely sure of their sounds.

*July 20th.* Showed Gwynneth how the sound for 'in' is made up of the sounds for 'i' and 'n'.

*July 21st.* Showed Gwynneth how the sound for 'it' is made up of the sounds for 'i' and 't'.

*July 22nd and following days.* Continued fitting sounds to two-letter words.

*July 23rd.* Finished vocabulary and pages for *Who Are You?* Gwynneth read the same book in small print. Finished alphabet.

*July 25th.* Gwynneth learned the words she didn't know for *Play With Us*. She then read the book all the way through.

*July 26th.* Began learning the sounds for the combinations. Began learning words for *The Three Little Pigs* (Follett): about 14 new words. Learning four words a day.

*July 27th.* Gwynneth finished learning words for *The Three Little Pigs*. (She had picked up several of the new words beforehand.) She read the book all the way through.

*July 28th.* Began learning the words for *The Three Goats*: 8 new words.

*July 29th.* Finished learning words for *The Three Goats* and read the book.

*July 30th.* Learned words for *The Funny Baby*: 5 new words. And read the book.

*July 31st.* Learned words for *The Three Bears* — and read it. Finished analysing the 12 two-letter words.

*August 1st.* Began learning words for *We Have Fun*: 11 new words. Began playing the building game with three-letter words.

*August 5th.* Finished reading *We Have Fun.*

*August 6th.* Began learning vocabulary for 'Going Camping', another homemade loose-leaf book about our coming holiday: 25 new words.

*August 9th.* Finished 'Going Camping'.

*August 10th–25th.* Away on holiday.

*August 29th.* Finished reading *Things We Like*: 11 new words. Began reading *Ten Apples Up On Top*: 27 new words. Finished playing the building game with the 30 three-letter words.

(During the following month, Gwynneth read on her own *The Zoo*, *The Farm*, and *Numbers* — all Ladybird Learning To Read Series — asking me what each unfamiliar word said until she had learned them all. I showed her how the sounds for the regular words were built up.)

*September 1st.* Finished learning the sounds for the combinations. In the following days, Gwynneth, copying me, learned to build up the sounds for 'hop', 'stop', 'drop' and others.

*September 6th.* Finished *Ten Apples Up On Top*. Gwynneth has a reading vocabulary of 275 words.

*September 7th.* Began reading *Are You My Mother?*: 18 new words. Began writing up sound chart (ba, be, bi, bo, bu, etc.). In the following days, Gwynneth was able to translate new three-letter words by herself with the building game — 'sat', 'hen', etc.

*September 13th.* Finished *Are You My Mother?*

*September 14th.* Began reading *Green Eggs and Ham*: 12 new words. Gwynneth translated 'thank' (new word) and others.

*September 17th.* Finished *Green Eggs and Ham.*

*September 18th.* Began reading *The King, The Mice and The Cheese*: 66 new words. Gwynneth translated 'lived' (new word) and others.

*September 20th and following days.* Began showing Gwynneth how the magic 'ĕ' works. I built up the sounds of these words for her: 'made', 'wise', 'time' (which she could already read) and she was then able to build them up herself in the same way. She showed her dolls how to build up the sounds for these words.

Dropped her reading for a while and read *The King, The Mice and The Cheese* to her a few times. (See Chapter 4, 3.)

*October 3rd.* Gwynneth read *The King, The Mice and The Cheese* straight through.

*October 4th.* Began reading *A Fly Went By*: 37 new words. I am now putting only irregular words on the blackboard — as we meet regular words in the book, I build up their sounds for Gwynneth, or she builds them up herself. I am still uncovering the letters for her.

*October 9th.* Began reading *The Little Red Hen and The Grains of Wheat*. Gwynneth insisted on reading some of it by herself after I read it to her.

*October 11th.* Finished *A Fly Went By*.

*October 12th.* Finished *The Little Red Hen and The Grains of Wheat*. Began *A Fish Out of Water*. Gwynneth translated 'tail', 'indeed' and 'gave' (new words) by herself. *Gwynneth*: 'Gu, ga, gav.' *Mum*: 'What does the "ĕ" do to the "ă" — makes it into an — ?' *Gwynneth*: 'An "ā"!' *Mum*: 'That's right! So the word says — ?' *Gwynneth*: 'Gave!'

*October 13th.* Finished *A Fish Out of Water*. I am no longer putting any new words on the blackboard. Gwynneth has a reading vocabulary of at least 450 words. I read her *The*

*Gingerbread Boy*, casually pointing out difficult new words as I went along. Gwynneth began reading the book by herself. She had learned many of the new words as I read. When we reached others she could not remember, I told her the sounds for irregular words, and built up the sounds for some regular words for her. Other regular words she translated herself, with me uncovering the letters.

*October 14th.* I read *The Gingerbread Boy* to Gwynneth again, and she finished reading it herself.

*October 17th.* Gwynneth read *The Gingerbread Boy* again, all the way through, refusing to let me go until she had finished. She now knew virtually all the words, with very little hesitation. Later, I read *The Three Little Pigs* to her.

*October 18th and 19th.* We tackled *The Three Little Pigs* (Ladybird) in the same way as *The Gingerbread Boy*. By the time we finished, I had read the book to her three times, and she had read it to me twice. She read about halfway through the book at a time.

*October 20th–December 6th.* Read through *The Cat In the Hat Beginner Book Dictionary* (an invaluable learning book, and great fun): total vocabulary 1,350 words. Gwynneth did not learn all these, but she probably knew at least 1,000 by the time we finished. Some words were quite outside her experience, and if these didn't 'stick', we left them alone. Other words were completely new to her, but she had already had the experiences which enabled her to understand their meanings, and she learned their shape symbols and their sound symbols at the same time.

We read about five pages at a time, first in the morning, and then the same five pages again at bed-time. By this time she had learned almost all the new words. After a while we just went over the more difficult new words at bed-time. We didn't read every day.

Here are some of the new words which Gwynneth translated by herself as we went through the dictionary (sometimes I uncovered the letters, sometimes she did): corner, count, deep, fork, free, fresh, frown, cards, garden, hanger, honk, inch, ink, itch, keep, kissed, luck, mail, mask, match, meat, meet, often, part, party, pedal, rode, rooster, scooter, sale, shut, shutters, sniff, fetch, stone, towel, turkey, uncle, valley, vanilla, wag, wagon, week, whisker, yelps, zipper. She could translate any verb or adjective she knew, with common endings added (-ed, -ing, -er, -est). Usually, I did not ask her to translate words whose meaning was unfamiliar, but she sometimes tackled such words of her own accord.

She could also read aloud, straight away, many of the simple words which I had never taught her, and which I was surprised to find that she knew. She could have learned them from Helen, who reads to her quite a bit, and the pictures helped too. But I am fairly certain that she was translating many of them into sounds at a glance, for she mispronounced some irregular words in accordance with their letter sounds (as she mispronounced 'soul' in 'Old King Cole'). 'Move' was at first read 'mohve', 'worm' was 'warm', and so on. But I have listed only the words whose sounds I knew she was building up then and there.

Now I have finished teaching Gwynneth to read. I don't plan to ask her to read to me regularly any more. Now she will go on in the same way as Helen: when I think she is ready to tackle something a bit more difficult, I will choose the most interesting book I can find, and begin by reading bits of it to her first. If it 'takes', she will

6

go through it on her own, although she will probably want me to finish reading it to her as well. If she doesn't like it, then I have chosen badly and must find something else. If she doesn't read a new book all the way through, it doesn't matter.

When your child has reached this point, don't worry too much about the reading level of his new books. Concentrate on choosing a book of the right *interest* level: something well written and well illustrated, that widens his experience just a little bit more. (Collections of nursery rhymes and songs will probably be popular with two-year-olds; nursery rhymes, poems, fairy tales and so on with threes and fours.) Good, clear print is important. If he likes the book you have chosen, in one way or another he will find out what the new words mean, and what they say. For by now you have closed the gap—and if he can understand it, he can read it.

# PART TWO

# Helping Children to Write

# 6

## Pros and Cons

For a long time it seemed to me that teaching a tiny child to write was a bad idea for various reasons. I doubted that a two-year-old, for example, would have sufficient control of pencil or chalk. I had mental images of school children poring over sheets of paper, tongues sticking out in concentration, making the same shape again and again, finally rushing off with a sense of release when writing time was over. Well, that could wait for school, thank you. I didn't see how writing could be taught without boring drill and exercises to develop ease and control.

Finally, Doman's recognition that reading written words is the other side of understanding spoken words, and probably shouldn't be linked with writing at first, seemed very important. Reading could clearly be regarded as natural for tiny children—but to force small hands through all kinds of unnatural contortions, when they would be so much better occupied pushing trains, building with blocks, hanging on to swings, seemed a genuine intrusion into childhood.

So it was not until Helen was getting on for five years old that I decided she might as well make a beginning. I knew that she would have enough manual control by this time, for she had been tracing over the letters on the blackboard for quite a while; she would soon be going to school, and might as well have some idea of what writing was all about before she went, and I had long finished teaching her to read, so there was no risk of confusing her. I felt I could teach her quite a lot in five minutes a day, which was hardly robbing her playtime.

Now I was in for a surprise. Helen enjoyed learning to write, and could soon write her name by herself. But Gwynneth (nearly three) saw me playing a new, fascinating game with Helen, and became highly indignant at being left out. When a small and angry person grabs a piece of chalk and threatens tears if she isn't helped to write a word on the blackboard like her sister, you don't argue or explain that she's too little. You give in gracefully and humour her for the sake of family harmony. As she could already read fluently, I did not think that writing could do any harm.

The result was that I found myself teaching both children to write at the same time. Helen had more control than Gwynneth, although there was not so big a difference here as I had expected. But Gwynneth, as with reading, enjoyed learning more, and took just as much pride in the words she had written.

After this had gone on for some weeks, and Gwynneth was not only tracing over my outlines, but also trying, of her own accord, to write words by herself, I began to wonder if two or three might not be a more natural age than five plus for children to learn to write.

I sat down and thought about my former objections.

1. A tiny child does not have sufficient control of pencil or chalk.

Different children develop control at different ages. But at some time during their third year, most children can draw a fairly round head and add a couple of pairs of sticks for arms and legs. If you analyse the letters of the alphabet, you will see that every one, capital and lower case, is nothing but curved lines or straight lines, or a combination of the two. So if a child can draw a curve and a straight line, he can, theoretically, learn to combine variations of these in all the ways necessary to produce the letters of the alphabet. (And if he cannot draw a curve and a straight line, then obviously he isn't ready to learn to write.) I decided that control was not really the problem.

2. The real question is: Why should a child *want* to do all these 'unnatural' things? If writing were natural for a tiny child, wouldn't he learn to write by himself, just as he learns to gain control over a spoon, a knife and fork, the buttons on his shirt?

As I thought over this one, the answer seemed to be: perhaps he will. After all, he learns to wield a knife because the knife is *there*; because he sees his parents using knives; because his mother helps him to hold one, sometimes presses her hand down over his own so that *he* cuts the potatoes. If he had no experience of knives and forks, it would never occur to him to try to handle them himself.

Until very recently, most tiny children have had no direct experience of written words. They have seen their parents writing letters—and often they have produced their own 'letters' in imitation: sheets of paper with wiggly lines going from side to side. They haven't tried to write words because words have meant nothing to them. But now that the reading revolution is gathering momentum, this situation is changing. And I think it would be surprising if many a child who learns to read at home does not try, quite spontaneously, to copy his mother and make the words that she makes. If this happens, why shouldn't she encourage him and show him exactly how to make the letters he wants to make, just as she guides his hand when he's trying to cut potatoes?

The more I thought about it, the more my former doubts about teaching writing seemed to dwindle. I began to see my objections in a different light. Why object to a child's learning to write, and not, say, to his washing up (we shouldn't inflict dreary chores like that on our children); or polishing the furniture with real polish (time enough for that when he has a home of his own); or making pastry with real flour and fat and putting it in the oven to bake (he'll have to cook in earnest soon enough)? But of course these are all things he adores to do, and he would happily spend much more time on them than Mum feels able to allow. Doman points out that much of a child's play is imitation of his parent's doings, and has the serious purpose of helping him grow up. Is writing really any more 'unnatural' than these other activities?

Other doubts are sometimes raised. When the pros and cons of early learning were discussed in various news media in the U.S., one objection was that a child who spent his early years on 'school subjects' should really be learning something far more important—how to get on with other people.

I find this an odd argument. The ability to establish satisfying human relationships is more important than any amount of skills, but why should we suppose that not learning one thing helps us to learn something else better? A child's most important relationship in the pre-school years is the relationship with his mother. It takes quite a long time for him to learn to play in co-operation with other children—to give a combined tea-party for the dolls, or to decide that someone is going to be the doctor, someone is going to be the patient. This sort of friendly play cannot be hurried or forced—or taught, in any direct sense. A mother simply tries to make sure that her child can be with other children as often as possible, and doesn't interfere too much when he is. In fact, Doman found out that when a mother teaches her child to read, they both enjoy it so much that their relationship benefits. When this fundamental human relationship is enriched, the results cannot be anything but good. If writing can be just as much fun as reading for mother and child, then it will only add to the pleasure they find in each other.

My last objection vanished when I realized that writing could be taught as naturally as reading, without any need for pressure, boredom, or meaningless drill—and that an enjoyable approach would probably be easier for a mother teaching one child than for a teacher coping with a whole herd. I describe one way of going about it in the next chapter.

Doman raises the question: when is the best age for a child to learn anything?—and gives the obvious answer: when he wants to. Given the chance, a child wants to learn to read when he is very small. It seems likely that once written words have become familiar friends, he will also want to learn to make them himself, and if we ignore his interest, he may not be nearly so enthusiastic later on.

To sum up: if, when you have taught your child to read, he wants to learn to write, and you want to teach him to write, then it cannot do any harm, and this may well be the best time for him to learn.

# 7

---

## Learning to Write

### I. 'Writing readiness'

How will you know when your child is able to form the letters, and how will you know when he wants to?

This is something you can leave to him. If you have been using a blackboard to teach him to read, his words are written on it in good big letters, and they stay there for as long as he needs them. Whenever he wants to, he can look at them, read them, scribble over them — and rub them off. (That is fun, too, and you don't need to discourage it. If you need to, you can write up the words again later.)

One day, all by himself, he will pick up a piece of chalk, and try to go over the shapes of the letters you have written. (Both Helen and Gwynneth did this quite early on, but as I have said, I paid little attention.) Wait for this development. I think it would be unwise to try to force his interest. When it happens, he has told you everything you need to know. He can control the chalk sufficiently to make the necessary shapes. And he wants to learn to make them.

### II. When to begin

It is a good idea, though, to finish teaching him to read before you make a real beginning with writing, if the reading sessions are going to be over within a few months. Then there will be no risk of confusing him by focusing attention on the shape-descriptions of the letters before he is certain of their sound-names. He will enjoy writing more when he can read well, for when he tries to write a word he will know exactly what it is that he is trying to reproduce. Success gives him great pleasure: he discovers that he can make these exciting symbols himself. A child who is just beginning to read may trace over some of the letters out of curiosity, but he is not so aware of the significance of what he is doing. Let your child go on experimenting by himself for a bit, which he will enjoy. When you have finished teaching him to read, you will probably feel that it has all ended much too soon, and it will be nice to have something to fill the gap!

But use your own judgment. Maybe you are planning to spend more than a few months teaching him to read. Then, so long as he is reading easily and with enjoyment, and the sounds of the letters are completely familiar, there is no harm in going ahead with writing when you want to.

You may wonder, why help him at all? Why not leave everything to him? You will be surprised to find how much he does learn by himself. But you need to help him learn how to make the letter shapes as exactly as possible, in the most efficient way, and how to align the tops and bottoms of his letters. He will take pleasure in your interest and help, and this will make him want to go on trying by himself. If nobody encourages his efforts after a while, he may give up before he has learned very much.

## III. Using a blackboard

If you don't have a blackboard, how will he show you when he is ready?

I must admit that I think a blackboard is essential for

writing, and that without one it would be better not to make the attempt. A child can make big, satisfying letters on a blackboard. He has almost boundless space for scribbling, and when he needs more, erasing is easy. He can write on a blackboard any time he wants to.

But if you are relying on paper and crayons, the initiative cannot really come from him. If you write his name on a piece of paper and suggest that he should sit down and try to crayon over the letters, he probably won't want to just then, and if you try to make him, you are dragging in all the old formal impositions. If you leave the paper lying around, he may not think of crayoning the letters before he has drawn faces all over the paper, or used it to wrap up presents for his dolls. If he does have a try, somehow he will have to hold the paper steady while he crayons. Even if he gets this far, it will be much more difficult for him to learn to control the shapes of the letters when he is crouched over a flat surface than if he is standing at a vertical one.

We may find that a blackboard does for writing what huge print has done for reading, and for the same reason: it provides the right materials at the right time.

(For writing, it should be a fixed, straight-up-and-down board, rather than a sloping, moveable one.)

## IV. Writing skills

Before you begin, think about the skills that are involved in writing. There are really only two. As we have already seen, a child needs to be able to draw a straight line and a curved line. Secondly, he needs to be able to direct these lines so that they begin at a particular point and end at a particular point. Any activity which develops these two skills helps him to learn to write.

This means, for example, that you do not need to teach

him to write each individual letter of the alphabet, one after the other. Help him to make just the letters that interest him. Maybe he will want to make the same word every day, for many days. By the time he can reproduce it on his own, he may be able to manage most of the other letters without much help. Perhaps he chooses a different word every day, although you feel he has not mastered the letters in other words he has attempted. He is still practising the same basic shapes, and learning to make them go more exactly where he wants them to go.

## V. The basic shapes

Next, examine the various shapes which combine to make all the letters. Again, these are comparatively few. It isn't necessary to teach your child to make these isolated shapes, one by one, or persuade him to practise the same shape over and over until he can do it neatly. That takes you right back to drill and formal exercises. But it will help if you have a name or description for each shape, so that you can show him how the same shape occurs in different letters, and help him to visualize what is needed.

Choose any names that will appeal to your child. Don't teach him these names before you begin. He will learn them gradually, as you talk about the letters you are making together. Here are the descriptions we used:

*Straight lines, or sticks.* l (as in b, h): a big Daddy-sized stick. l (as in i, a): a Helen-sized stick. - (as in e, f, t): a stick going crossways, or (as in J, G): a straight hat. \ (as in v, w): a stick leaning over this way. / (as in v, w): a stick leaning over that way.

*Curves.* 'O', the sound, 'ŏ'. 'C' (as in c, d): the sound, 'cu'. (As these shapes are letters in their own right, we simply used names which were already familiar.) ɔ (as in b, p): a big fat tummy. ⌒ (as in f, r): a roundy hat. ⌐ (as in n, m): a poor old bent women. ∪ (as in u): a cup. ‿ (as in J, g, y): a tail.

You don't begin by teaching your child to make these shapes by themselves, or single letters, for the same reason that you didn't teach him to read by beginning with the alphabet. Words are what interest him. He will enjoy learning to write whole words, but if you keep to single letters, he will get bored.

## VI. Writing sessions

Your child has begun by tracing over words already on the blackboard, not by copying them. Keep to this approach indefinitely. During most of the writing sessions, he will go over outlines that you draw for him, rather than make separate copies of his own. He will move on to copying when he is ready. For the time being, you are simply guiding his own efforts so that he learns to begin the shapes at the most convenient place, make them in the best order and the best direction, and line up the tops and bottoms.

The first writing session—like all the rest—will be very simple.

Help your child to choose a word he finds interesting. His own name is probably best of all. You could write it on the blackboard and leave it there for several days before you start.

One morning, say: 'Let's write your name, shall we? Would you like to write it for me?' and you draw three horizontal lines, parallel, on the board. Explain that the top line is for the tops of tall letters, the middle line is for the tops of short letters, and the bottom line is for the letters to sit on. (A good size to aim at would be the size of the words in the Doman 'self' vocabulary—about $2\frac{1}{4}$ inches between the middle line and the bottom line. A learner finds it much easier to write big letters than small ones.)

Now draw the first shape for the first letter, slowly and carefully, explaining what you are doing, and where the stroke begins and ends. Let your child go over this same shape with his piece of chalk, making sure that he begins where you began and ends where you did. Describe the shape again as he makes it. Your strokes should be quite faint, in a pale colour, and his bolder, in a bright colour, so that *his* word is clearly visible. Help him to add the next shape to the letter in the same way, and when he has finished, ask him to tell you what letter he has written. (Go on using the sounds of the letters rather than their names.) Help him to write the other letters in a similar way.

Suppose, for example, that your child's name is James. The session will go something like this:

*Mum*: 'I'm going to begin by making a capital "Ju". We need a capital "Ju", not just an ordinary one, because it is the first letter of your name, and your name is a very important word. First I make a big Daddy-sized stick, from the very top line down to the bottom line, and then I put a little tail for it to sit on. You make the big Daddy-sized stick. Yes, that's right – begin at the top line. Now go down and down, making the stick – and there's the tail for him to sit on. Very good – very good! Now, look – I'm going to put a little straight hat on the top, like this. You go over it. That's right – there's his hat! Now, what letter have you made?

'Let's make an "a" now. An "a" is just a "cu" with a James-sized stick, isn't it? Here is how I make a "cu". I start here – and he goes round with his top touching the middle line. Round he goes – round he goes, and now he's sitting on the bottom line. You do that. That's right, begin over there. Good, you're making his top touch the middle line. Now he's going round—and round—really he should sit on the bottom line, like Mummy's, but that's very good. Now I'm going to put on a James-sized stick—like this. It starts at the middle line and goes down to the bottom. What letter have you made now? And what does the word say now? Ja—all right, what letter do we want next?

'Here is how I make a "mu". It begins with a James-sized stick, from the middle line down to the bottom line. Can you go over it? Yes, from the middle line straight down to the bottom. Now here comes a poor old bent woman—like this. Look, here's her head—and her back goes up and touches the middle line, and now she's standing on the bottom line. You make her. No, start her head just there— look, that's it. Now make her back go up—and round— now you're making her stand on the bottom line. Very good! That's a "nu", isn't it—now we're going to make it into a "mu". We just put another bent old woman here— like this. Up, and round, and now she's standing on the bottom line. You make her as well. That's it, that's it! Now what letter have you made? What does the word say so far? "Jam"! Well, now we need a magic "ē", don't we, to make it say "Jame".

'I start over here, and make a stick going crossways. You go over it. That's right—a crossways stick. Now I shall just put a "cu" on to the stick—like this. You make the "cu" now. That's right—make it touch the middle line and go round and sit on the bottom. Now we've made the word say—what? Jame!

'Well, we need just one more letter, don't we—what is it? "Su"—a really wiggly one. I begin here, and make a *tiny* "cu". He just goes half the way down. You go over it. Then we put on a *little* fat tummy going the other way, sitting on the bottom line. You make the little fat tummy. That's

right, round he goes, on to the bottom line. There you are —
what letter is that? So what word have you written? Yes,
you've written your name! Aren't you clever! Wait till we
tell Daddy! We'll have to leave it on the blackboard, so we
can show him when he gets home. Oh, you're a clever boy!'

In practice, this will have taken about five minutes, and
your child will almost certainly be vastly pleased with himself by the time you have finished. Stop there. Don't ask him
to go over his name again, or write another word. He has
made a very good beginning.

The next day, spend five minutes on another writing
session, again asking him to choose a word. (Help him to
want to join in by saying: 'What word shall we write today?'
rather than just: 'Do you want to do some writing?')
Always let him choose the word he wants to write, although
you may suggest words for him to consider. (Names of
other members of the family, friends and dolls should be
popular.) He will be more interested in a word he has chosen
himself. You do not need to feel that you should select words
so as to cover all the letters of the alphabet, because, as I
have said, even if he chooses the same word day after day,
he is still practising the two basic skills which will soon
enable him to write any letter when he wants to. The most
important thing about each writing session is not the particular letters that he learns to make, but that he should enjoy
it, and want to go on. It is when he is experimenting by
himself that he will really learn to write.

It is a good idea to write the word he chooses at the top of
the blackboard before you begin the session, so that, as he
completes each letter, he can tell you what letter comes
next.

Handle the second session in just the same way as the first
session, describing each stroke as you make it, pointing out

7

where it begins and ends, and repeating your explanation as your child makes the stroke himself. (Go on doing this even when a letter has become quite familiar.) Play the building game with him as each letter is added, so that he remembers he is writing letters, and not just drawing arrangements of curves and sticks.

Suppose he chooses to write 'James' many times during the next few weeks, until he is making the strokes quite easily. Notice how many other letters he will now be able to make, simply by combining the same shapes in different ways: b, c, d, g, h, i, j, l, n, p and t—as well as half the capitals.

Again, there is no need to teach capital letters by themselves. Teach them naturally, during the writing sessions, by beginning several words with capital letters. Point out the capitals as you make them, and explain that they come only at the beginnings of words. You could say that some words, like names, are always very important, and always begin with capital letters. Other words usually begin with ordinary letters; but they are important when they are at the beginning of ideas, and then they begin with capital letters as well. Point this out to your child the next time you read him a story (point out the full stop as well if you want, and explain that it usually comes at the end of an idea). He may not understand this explanation all at once, but it will fall into place later on, when he is writing sentences, and you need to explain that he should not use a capital letter any time he feels like it. It may be useful to contrast 'capital' letters with 'ordinary' letters, so as to reserve 'big' and 'little' for variations in size.

To sum up your approach in each writing session:

1. Let your child choose the word to write. Write it at the top of the blackboard before you begin.

2. Don't ask him to make a separate copy; ask him to trace over your outlines.

3. Say if you are beginning with a capital letter.

4. Make one stroke at a time.

5. Describe each stroke as you make it, pointing out where it begins and ends.

6. Describe the stroke in the same way as your child goes over it.

7. Play the building game as each letter is added.

8. Praise him enthusiastically as you go along.

9. One word each day is usually enough.

That is really all there is to it, and you can go on following this approach indefinitely. If at times he doesn't feel like writing, leave it alone for a few days.

Keep on making just one stroke at a time, rather than a complete letter, for a long while. When you think your child is thoroughly familiar with a particular letter, try making the whole outline before he goes over it. ('S's and lower-case 'e's will become single continuous outlines fairly soon.) But if his letter wanders badly off the tracks when he tackles a complete outline, or if he forgets where each stroke begins, or its direction, go back to building that letter stroke by stroke. In fact, there is no harm in keeping to this single stroke method for many letters until he is copying by himself. You want him to be so certain of the way to make the strokes that they come naturally when he is writing on his own. When he is copying words, he may go on taking the chalk away from the board at the end of each stroke. He will learn to make letters like 'b's and 'm's in one continuous movement later on, when he needs to write faster because he has more words he wants to write. If he needs help at that point, you can show him how to keep the chalk on the board or the pencil on the paper until the letter is completed.

## VII. Copying words

Copying words, rather than going over their outlines, is again something you can leave to him. Then you will be certain that you are not hurrying him on to something he is not ready for, or does not want to do. Leave interesting words on the blackboard to encourage him, even though he is not learning to read new words from the board any more. Perhaps you can ask him to tell you a story he loves or has made up, and write up one of his sentences as he says it. He is bound to be interested in something he has generated, and if one day he tries to copy one of these sentences, he may well keep going until he has finished it.

His letters will probably go a bit wild when he is copying rather than tracing. Concentrate on praising his efforts and showing your excitement about what he is doing, rather than criticizing. Some criticism can be offered as help and encouragement: 'Shall I draw some lines for your letters to sit on? That's a very good "nu" — it's *nearly* as tall as the "a". Next time I expect you'll make it just as tall. Aren't you doing well!' This sort of approach shows your child what is wrong, and makes him want to make the letters even better next time, without dampening his pride and pleasure at all.

Keep on making outlines for him to go over every day — maybe still one stroke at a time — even when he has begun copying by himself. This gives him the practice he needs in making the letters exactly. When you are sure his control is very good, you can start asking him to copy a word during each writing session, instead of tracing it.

(Don't feel, by the way, that in the writing sessions you must give him the chance to make mistakes, so that he will learn from them. Very often children don't learn anything from their mistakes except how to go on making them! When you were teaching him to play the building game, you simply made it as difficult as possible for him to go wrong. The same principle applies here. This way he never feels that writing is a struggle, and every success gives him the confidence to go on.)

By this time, he is probably writing on various bits of paper, as well as on the board. He will be able to handle paper and pencil more easily, now that he knows what he is doing. His name is likely to turn up in all sorts of places! He may like to write his name on his books, and sign letters to Granny. This can gradually be extended to sentences and short paragraphs. Let him tell you what he wants to say; you tell him the letters that he needs. He may go on telling you stories to put on the blackboard, and copying these sentences. After a while, you can encourage him to copy these into his own special writing book.

In fact, if you sit back and think about it, you have taught him to write. Or rather, you have helped him to learn to write. From beginning to end, there has been no coercion, no drill, no exercises. These were unnecessary because learning to write wasn't really your idea, anyway. It was his idea, and he has moved ahead so quickly because you didn't impose writing as a task. You merely helped him to do something he wanted to do.

## VIII. A writing alphabet

Here is an alphabet with simple letter forms you could use as models. Your child can probably recognize simplified **a** and **g** by now, but if not, teach him to recognize them by using them in 'reading' words on the blackboard before showing him how to write them.

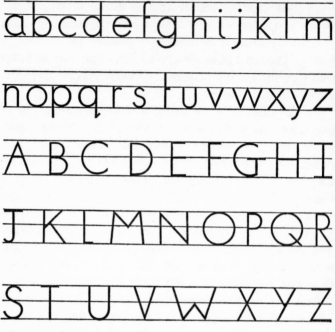

Notice that it is easier to make straight strokes downwards, and the following letters may be printed as shown:

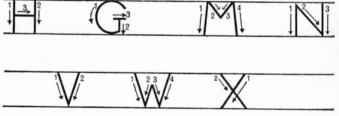

In the case of 'K' and 'k', it is probably better to make the second stroke upwards, to make sure that it joins the vertical stroke at the proper place.

# 8

## Spelling

The child who spells well is not the child who has learned a great many rules about spelling, but the child who reads a lot. Almost without thinking about it he visualizes the words he needs, and when he has written them, he can tell whether or not they 'look' right.

So we can assume that the way a child sees words as he reads plays quite a large part in the way he spells them.

Once again, teachers on each side of the alphabet battle have accused the other side of fostering poor spelling, and once again, I think, both are right.

A child who sees words mainly as symbols, as meanings, may have difficulty with spelling because he hasn't had much practice in consciously breaking down words into their constituent letters. He may be aware that a word 'looks' wrong without being able to identify the particular letter which needs alteration.

On the other hand, a child who has tackled reading by beginning with the alphabet, and working out words from their shape-sounds, may spell badly because he is apt to 'hear' the words he writes (instead of visualizing them), and he spells by translating these sounds into shapes. He may spell something like this: 'On Wensday we hav a speling lessun.'

If you teach your child reading and phonetics in the way I suggest, I think you will find that he will have little difficulty with spelling. From the beginning, the shape of the word, the way it looks, will receive more emphasis than the corresponding sound. This will help your child to form the habit of visualizing the words he writes, rather than concentrating on their sounds. Then you will prevent his having difficulty in identifying each separate part of a shape-word, by teaching him phonetic analysis. Each letter will still receive more emphasis than its corresponding sound, because you teach phonetics by analysing words your child can already read, until the habit of analysis spreads to unfamiliar words. As he progresses with phonetic analysis, he will absorb a great deal of conscious information about how the words he sees are made up, and about their wrinkles and peculiarities.

When he is writing independently, you can help him to acquire the habit of spelling correctly. Once again, guide the bicycle until he can cope by himself. Don't make him try to remember how to spell the words he wants to write; just tell him the letters he needs. The more often he spells words correctly now, the more often he will spell them correctly later on. The more mistakes he makes now, the more mistakes he will make later on. He learns how to spell correctly by seeing the words he writes, properly spelled.

Of course, you can encourage him to decide which letters he needs, while making sure that he decides on the right ones! Ask him to look at the word inside his head, and try to 'see' the letter that comes next.

If he is writing a regular word, you can use his knowledge of its shape-sounds to help him visualize the word. Play the building game with him. Suppose he tells you that he wants to write 'bad'. 'Well,' you can say, 'first you want to make the word say "bu".' 'All right, I've made a "bu". What comes then, Mummy?' 'Well, now make the word say "ba". What letter do you need?' 'Oh, an "ă". All right, "ă". Now what?' 'Now make the word say "bad".' 'Oh, "du". I've done it, Mummy! I've written "bad"!'

If he is writing a very irregular word, like 'cough', and he cannot yet visualize it on his own, simply tell him the letters and do not bother with the building game.

If he is writing a word with occasional wrinkles, use both approaches. Here, for example, is Gwynneth tackling 'write' and 'garage', two words she insisted on writing the other day.

'How do I do "write", Mummy?'

'First you need a "wu".'

'I've made a "wu". What comes next?'

'Now you want a "ru".'

' "Ru". What comes next?'

'Well, make it say "ri". What letter do you think?'

'Oh, an "ĭ". All right. What's next?'

'Now make it say "rit".'

' "Tu"! I've made a "tu".'

'Well, now you need a magic "ĕ", to make the "ĭ" into an "ī".'

'Oh, a little magic "ĕ". I've done it, Mummy. I've made "write". Come and look!'

Then for some unknown reason she decided to write 'garage', and here is Mum helping. 'Make the word say "gu". Now make it say "ga". You want a "ru" to make it say "gar". Now make it say "gara". Now you want a "gu". Now the word says "garag", so you need a magic "ĕ" to make the "gu" into a "ju".'

'I've done it, Mummy! I've written "garage"! Come and see!'

You may feel that by taking charge of your child's spelling in this way, you will be stifling his initiative and creativity, but this is not so. Your child is not remotely interested in being a good speller, as such, and he won't be until he feels the pressures of social conventions. What interests him is watching his thoughts take shape on paper, and seeing that the words he writes look just like the ones he loves to read. He is intensely engaged in thinking about what he wants to say, and in choosing the words he needs to say it. He is having the time of his life, and you are helping him to enjoy it by not bothering him about the mechanical side of the operation.

What our children are aware of learning, and what we are aware of teaching, may not always be the same thing, and that is a very comfortable arrangement.

*The initial teaching alphabet*

Where spelling is concerned, I think that once again the use of the initial teaching alphabet puts a school child at a disadvantage. At the age of eight or more, he is gradually removed from his safe, regular, ordered cocoon, and finds himself face to face with 'English as she is writ'. He may have little difficulty in reading the new language, but he now has to begin trying to visualize the new spelling, in all its oddities and quirks. He will find this doubly difficult, because the i.t.a. has probably encouraged him to spell words from their sounds, rather than from the way they look, and because he has not been able to store up mental images of irregular words. Or, indeed, of most words as they are normally spelled.

At an age when it is becoming more difficult, not less, for him to learn language – at an age when language should be for him a precision instrument, honed through years of familiarity and use, capable of responding to all his needs of thought and expression, without his having to wrestle with its mechanics—*now* he has to begin worrying about *spelling*.

Some backers of the initial teaching alphabet even advocate using the medium more widely than as just a teaching aid. Since it is so much more 'logical' and 'rational' than 'traditional orthography', with its so-called perversities of spelling, they claim that it should eventually replace ordinary spelling entirely, making life easier for everyone.

The recognition that written words are symbols in their own right, without any necessary dependence on spoken words, helps us to see that this is a monstrous proposal. It is just because written English is *not* a completely faithful phonetic translation of speech that written words can convey a richness of meaning which is not always apparent from the sounds alone. The difference in meaning between two words which *sound* the same is sometimes revealed in the *spelling*. (There, their; oral, aural, etc.) Common derivations of words, related prefixes, and so on, are often clearer in the spelling than in the saying (compare 'prēdetermine' and 'prĕjudice'); and written words can allude to whole skeins of meaning not immediately apparent from the spoken words. (This is one reason why written poetry is poetry in its own right, and not simply a pale representation of spoken verse.)

Written English words carry cargoes of meaning from other ages and from other languages. Over many years, human beings have laden them with the finest treasures of their minds. Why people like George Bernard Shaw and Sir James Pitman should want to jettison some of this cargo is beyond me.

We have adopted the i.t.a. because we have thought that

we make it easier for a child to learn by removing the complexities from what he learns, instead of concentrating on making it as easy as possible for him to master those complexities.

Perhaps our fundamental mistake has been to suppose that when a child learns to read, write and spell, he should also be learning *how* to learn. He should, we feel, be learning how to tackle problems, how to try various solutions until he finds the right one, and how to work things out by himself.

But language should not be something a child has to think *about*. Language is what he thinks *with*. When he learns to solve problems, language brings him information about those problems (hearing and reading); language carries his attempts to come to grips with the problems (thinking); and language explains his solutions (speaking and writing). When he wants to think *about* language, he can go to university and study linguistics.

When we want our children to learn to solve problems, let's give them jigsaw puzzles and bricks, let's teach them maths, let's encourage them to attempt scientific experiments. But don't let us make them practise problem-solving on something as fundamental as their use of language.

When we teach them reading, writing and spelling, let's forget about teaching them how to learn, and let's just teach them to read, write and spell.

# PART THREE

## The Revolution in the Classroom

PART II

# 9

## The Revolution in the Classroom

Mothers who have used Doman's teaching methods with their two-year-olds have watched, almost with unbelief, while the children soak up whole words at fantastic rates. Doman's explanation for this rapid learning is that a baby's ability to absorb knowledge is enormous, and that it decreases rather than increases as he grows older. This is why, he says, a school child learns to read so much more laboriously than a baby.

But since Doman's approach makes reading enjoyable and natural for a toddler, might it not have the same effect for older children? And since it rests on a different, illuminating theory of written language, should we not expect that theory to have ramifications in the classroom as well as in the home? Isn't it even possible that when the theory is properly applied in the classroom, school children will learn to read much more rapidly than they do at present?

At this point, some educationists would disagree. Doman's method, they maintain, is nothing but the old 'look-and-say' which has been tried extensively, and discredited, in the schools.

I do not believe that Doman's ideas and methods of presentation *have* been tried in the schools to any great extent.

When they are, in the full understanding of what is actually happening when a child reads, the change that results will, I think, make all the difference.

In order to show this clearly, I would like to examine the imaginary case of Johnny, who lives in a strange country where children are not exposed to spoken language at home, but do learn to read – that is, to understand written language – from an early age.

When he is five, Johnny goes to school, and the big problem which educationists, teachers and parents must then tackle is: 'How shall we teach Johnny to hear?' There is another important question, closely linked with this one, but not usually asked because its answer is taken for granted: 'How shall we *find out* whether or not Johnny can hear language?' The obvious answer is that we will know Johnny has heard a spoken word correctly when he is able to pick out the corresponding written word in response to it.

There are two main ways of teaching Johnny to hear. We can use the 'whole word' or 'hear-and-see' method. The teacher pronounces a new word, at the same time holding up a word card bearing the corresponding written word. Johnny can understand this written word, and gradually learns to associate the unfamiliar sound with the familiar shape. Then the teacher introduces the next spoken word. Progress is slow and thorough.

Hearing lessons take up only a small part of Johnny's school day. The rest of the time he is building, modelling, playing, learning about numbers; and written language naturally accompanies these activities because it is so much easier for him to understand. The teacher's suggestions and remarks are flashed on to a screen at the front of the classroom.

Johnny's **mother** is discouraged from using spoken

language in the home, because this is likely to confuse and pressure Johnny, rather than help him.

After about four years of 'hear-and-see', Johnny can hear language almost as easily as he can read it. He has made average progress, and he has a 'hearing age' of nine.

The main disadvantage of the 'hear-and-see' method is that Johnny is always dependent on someone else to show him the written word that corresponds to the sound. This means that he will never be able to hear independently, for how can he be said to have learned a new spoken word unless he knows how it *looks*?

The second way of teaching Johnny to hear is the 'phonetic' method. Every spoken word is made up of individual sounds which have shape values, and if we teach Johnny to associate individual sounds with individual shapes, he will be able to match spoken words with written ones by himself. This method, used from the beginning, can be more laborious and frustrating for Johnny than 'hear-and-see', but it does teach him to find out how new spoken words look, more quickly than if he learned nothing but whole words. However, it is still three or four years before Johnny can hear language as easily and as 'comprehendingly' as he can see it.

When we invert written and spoken language like this, we can see how we would be mistaken to rely on *either* of the ways I have just outlined to teach Johnny to hear. But it is not the methods which are wrong. What are wrong are the assumptions on which the methods are based.

Supposing that we are still in this strange country where children learn to hear at school, how shall we alter our approach and help Johnny to hear in the shortest possible time? What mistakes have we made?

First, we have made the mistake of thinking that hearing

8

language is a difficult intellectual operation. Intellectual and sophisticated it may be, but a baby of less than a year can manage it easily.

Second, we have made the mistake of thinking that spoken language can be learned only in relation to written language. On the contrary, it is far more important to associate spoken words with their meanings than with their corresponding shapes. If Johnny can already read, the corresponding written word will be useful in building up the meaning for the spoken word. It will remind Johnny of the meaning, and help him to hear that meaning through the sound. But associating spoken words with written ones is only an *aid* to hearing language – it is not hearing itself.

Third, we have been more concerned about Johnny's ability to *prove* he can hear, by linking spoken words with written ones, than about the ways in which meaningful spoken language is presented to him. We should reverse the emphasis and stress teaching more than testing.

Fourth, we have made the mistake of thinking that Johnny will learn to hear better if we use only a little spoken language at a time, and that too free a use will confuse and pressure him. In fact he will learn much more easily if we surround him with a good deal of meaningful spoken language. Spoken language should accompany all his activities at school, and Johnny's mother should be encouraged to use speech freely in the home. We can go on bringing important words into sharp focus by relating these to written words, one at a time, but this activity should be seen as only a part of the whole. Once Johnny can hear fairly well, we can also help him to translate spoken words into shapes on his own, by teaching him phonetics. Again we should recognize that while this translation may help him to find out the meanings of unfamiliar spoken words which he can already read, it is a very different activity from hearing.

When we put right the mistakes that we have made, we will find that Johnny learns to hear more rapidly, easily and pleasurably – though he will not learn to hear language as quickly as he would have done as a baby.

Why should we make these changes in our 'hearing' methods? Not because we have decided that 'hear-and-see' is superior to the 'alphabetic' approach, but because we know that spoken language is *language* in its own right, and that its relationship to written language is separate from its power to symbolize ideas.

Let us climb back and take another look at language on the conventional side of the looking-glass: the side where the vast majority of children learn to hear at home, and to read at school. I suggest that Doman's ideas will entail exactly the same kind of changes in our basic assumptions about reading instruction. This is because Doman is not just advocating the 'whole word' approach as opposed to the 'alphabetic' approach. He is far more radical than that. Doman maintains that written language is *language*. A written word is a *word*.

And that idea alters *everything*.

How shall we begin teaching school children to read? Over the centuries, we have repeated this question, but we have not recognized that the answer to it depends on what we mean by *reading*.

Until now, we have usually supposed that in order to read a word, a child must be able to know what it *says*, and to recognize it whenever he meets it. Therefore, the first thing he must learn to do is to remember what a particular word says; and if he forgets it, he hasn't learned anything. Also, if saying a word is important, then the first words he learns to read should be easily translatable into sounds.

But if Doman is right, then the important thing about the initial stages of reading instruction is not that a child should be able to remember all the words he learns to read, nor that he should be able to say them, nor that he should be able to translate them into sounds by himself, *but that he should learn to see a word as a symbol, and to see a meaning through it*. Once he has achieved this, *he has learned to read*, and he can go on from there to read all the words that are made meaningful to him.

The early Doman vocabularies are lists of words denoting important objects or actions, in a child's world, and the child learns to read each one as an isolated word. This is not, in fact, the easiest way of *remembering* words. It is really easier to remember a word when we have met it several times in various sentences. As Helen and Gwynneth did not read these first Doman words in context fairly soon, they 'lost' quite a few, and when the words occurred later in story-books, several had to be relearned. This did not mean that learning the early vocabularies had been a waste of time. Helen and Gwynneth had been learning something far more important than the specific meaning of each word: they had been learning to see familiar ideas through written symbols, and to take great delight in interpreting these symbols. Everything that came later was built on this foundation.

Because reading words in context is a great aid to remembering them, many teachers approach reading instruction with the 'sentence method' or even the 'story method'. (They begin with a sentence or story, and only gradually focus attention on the individual words.) There are additional reasons for choosing the story method to begin with, which seem, at first sight, persuasive. Five-year-olds are more interested in stories than in isolated words. Many words — adjectives, adverbs, prepositions, conjunctions, certain forms of the verb — do not mean very much, taken alone. Also, if understanding written language is exactly comparable to understanding speech, isn't it sensible to use written language, from the beginning, as freely as speech, in the expectation that the children will learn to understand it in the same way?

These are good reasons for moving on to sentences and books fairly quickly, but not, I think, for *beginning* with sentences or stories. Starting with whole sentences rather than with single words has two disadvantages. If we want to help a child to read as efficiently as we can, we should present forms which he will come across frequently, rather than very infrequently. A sentence like 'One apple up on top' may never recur, but the separate words 'one', 'apple', 'up', 'on' and 'top' will recur hundreds of times in his early reading books. If we help him to read these words separately first, and then in combination, he will not only be able to read one sentence, but will also be well on the way to reading many other sentences which contain some of these words.

Also, the meaning of a sentence is a whole, but not an indivisible whole. It is formed by the dynamic relationships between the meanings of the words it contains, and a child reads a sentence when he sees the meanings of the separate words acting together to produce a complete thought. Unless he does this, he is not really reading. But once he *has* learned to see sentences in this way, even unfamiliar words can assume the glimmerings of meaning for him by virtue of their relationships to other words in the sentence.

And the analogy with spoken language may mislead us. Although a baby is conscious of a wide background of sound, we can probably assume that it is individual words which first emerge from this background with definite meanings – words like 'Mummy', 'Daddy', 'dog', 'baby'. If the baby never learned to distinguish particular words, his progress would be very slow; only as he is able to pick out the individual word can he understand the same word straight away, whenever he hears it. His growing understanding of spoken language broadens out from this base. As far as reading is concerned, I think we will save time and establish a solid foundation, if we do not wait for written words to emerge somewhat haphazardly from their context, but give them a hefty shove on the way. We should begin with isolated words, to make sure that the children really do learn to see a written shape as a symbol. Then the aim is to reach the natural level of a child's understanding as soon as possible. Since Helen was enjoying listening to stories when I began teaching her to read, I taught her to read books quite soon, and did not go through all the Doman vocabularies first. Gwynneth, over a year younger, spent more time learning isolated words. A one-year-old would spend longer still, since words interest him more than stories.

For any child, it is logical to concentrate on nouns first, since nouns do not depend on a context for a clear meaning, but can be taught by reference to easily identifiable objects.

Which nouns shall we choose?

If Doman is right, it is more important that the first words a child learns to read should be very *meaningful* to him, than that they should be easily translatable into sounds. When a child has not already formed a particular concept, or had the experiences which will enable that concept to be formed, to crystallize into shape together with the word, then the word will be a meaningless symbol to him. This is why it is more difficult for him to read the word 'fan', say, than the word 'mummy'. If he has never seen a fan, he can learn to 'read' the word only by 'look-and-say' — not by 'look-and-understand'.

Many teachers have recognized that it is easier for a child to associate a written shape with an interesting meaning than with an uninteresting one, or with a meaningless sound. Sylvia Ashton-Warner, who taught Maori children in New Zealand, developed a brilliantly successful teaching method which rested on this principle. She did not make Doman's final step, and recognize that a written word is a *word* in its own right, but her achievements certainly lend support to Doman's ideas. In her book *Teacher*, one of the most moving descriptions of the art of teaching I have read, she describes how she built up a close understanding with each child. As the child's trust grew, he and his teacher together were able to find words which were so meaningful to him that he was able to remember them when he had seen them only *once*.

Although Doman does not know most of the children whom he helps, through their mothers, to read, it was easy for him to draw up a word list which any mother could use, because every baby wants to learn the names for his various bits. By the time children get to school, they are beyond the stage of fascination with their ears, eyes, arms, legs and toes. So it is probably better not to begin with the Doman vocabularies in the classroom.

*Classroom methods*

But we should keep to Doman's underlying idea, and start off by selecting one word which will be important to every child in the room. We could pick the word 'school', since beginning school is a momentous happening for each child.

If this is the word the teacher chooses, then, after some friendly conversation about school involving as many children as possible, she writes the word 'school' in thick, bright, lower-case letters on the blackboard. She explains: 'This word says "school".' The word stays on the blackboard for the rest of the day, and the teacher points it out, in the same way, at intervals.

Two or three days later, the word is rubbed off, and another—possibly 'teacher'—is written in its place. Again, conversation centres around 'teacher', and the teacher reads the word aloud every now and then. By the end of the week, the children should be able to read both words, and distinguish between them. 'School' and 'teacher' go to sit at the top of the blackboard indefinitely, so that each child can look up and read the words any time he feels like it.

The most important task has been accomplished. The children can understand written symbols, and distinguish between one written symbol and another.

Now let names, in big red letters, be pasted on everything in the classroom where there is room for a label. This will be more fun if the children do the pasting. The lettering on the labels should be as big and bold as possible (lower-case 'a's $2\frac{1}{4}$ inches high). The 'lesson' might go something like this:

'Everyone bang his desk. Go on, make a big noise. Right, now this word' (holding up a label) 'says "desk". Who wants a card just like this to paste on his desk? I've got lots so you can all have one if you want.

'Doreen, where is the window? Go and touch it for me. This word says "window". "Window." You get some paste and glue the label on to the window, will you?

'What's this, Derek? A lamp? All right, here's a word that says "lamp". You stick it on.

'Who wants a word that says "door"? There are only two doors, so there are only two cards.'

And so on, over a period of a few days, until every nameable object in the room has a label, and the children can read these names any time they wish.

Each child should have a card with his Christian name printed on both sides. This card should be pasted on to his desk so that it stands upright, to enable the other children to read it from a distance. Meanwhile, the teacher could be finding out which words are particularly meaningful to each child, and giving him his own special word cards to keep.

Now she can move on to simple sentences, using the children's names, and making little stick drawings on the blackboard to add interest. Important Key Words such as 'here', 'and', 'is' and 'are' can be taught first, as isolated words. Later use in the sentences will bring out their meanings more clearly. 'Here is Alan.' 'Here is Sue.' 'Here are Alan and Sue.' These sentences can remain on the blackboard for a few days. The teacher reads them aloud to the children every now and then, pointing to each word as she does so.

The use of written language should not be limited to the 'reading lesson'. Simple words and sentences can be increasingly used as an accompaniment to *all* the children's activities. Remarks which the teacher makes frequently, like 'Time for break', 'Time for games', 'Get out the building blocks', 'Who wants the coloured paper?' can be written on the board as they are said. Then the teacher reads them aloud again, pointing to each word as she does so. Pictures of trees and flowers, all labelled with big words, can go up on the walls. If the children are using Colour Factor blocks for maths, pictures of the blocks, each one labelled with its name in big letters, can be pinned up. The children will probably enjoy pointing out these words and their meanings to each other every so often.

Notice that this clear, tempting use of written language is

not in the least likely to 'confuse' or 'pressure' the children. Nobody is being forced to read these words and sentences, or made to think that he has failed if he does not remember them. Written language is simply being presented as meaningfully as possible, and the children are not being prodded to *demonstrate* their ability to read it. They are only being encouraged to *absorb*.

The children begin to read books, using word cards as an aid to becoming really certain of the vocabulary in each book, and to recognizing capital letters and other variations. The Doman 'page by page' approach to the first book is most effective. Every day or so, a child is given a new page, which he clips into his folder. He may illustrate it himself. Every time a page is added, he rereads all the pages he has so far. The pages grow into a book before the child's eyes, giving him constant evidence of his progress.

Each child can make and illustrate his own book, dictating a story to the teacher who writes it down (simplifying if necessary), and makes word cards to go with the book. The books and cards can be passed around the class later on, for other children to read, with the author helping in case of difficulty.* These first books should be short, with a small vocabulary load.

If the teacher finds making word cards a chore, children in higher classes can be asked to help. This will give them a sensible and interesting reason for trying to print as neatly as possible, and it will also provide links between the younger and older children. Older ones could 'adopt' certain beginners, taking responsibility for their word cards, listening to them read books, and showing a general interest in their work. Even if the printing on the cards is a bit wobbly, this

* A similar approach was developed by Sylvia Ashton-Warner. See her book *Teacher*.

will not matter: there are more important things than perfect letters.

When the teacher needs to test a child's ability to recognize words, whether on cards or in books, she will often make it easier for him to respond by asking: 'Where is the word that says – ?' rather than: 'What is this word?' In several cases, I have found that a child who seems to have learned nothing when he is tested in the second way, shows that he can after all identify and distinguish between many words with this extra bit of help.

The class can contribute to a 'group story', which the teacher writes on the blackboard as each child adds his sentence. As before, the teacher should simplify, and tidy up the grammar if necessary. The teacher reads this story aloud to the children from time to time, again pointing to each word as she reads. In this way the children become thoroughly familiar with the way a sentence goes, and how to move from the end of one line to the beginning of the one underneath. They learn quite naturally that a capital letter marks the beginning, and a full stop the end of a thought-out idea; and that the sense of such an idea does not stop at the end of a *line*, but at the end of a sentence. The teacher can occasionally point this out.

Once a child can read, and follow the order of written words, the most rapid and efficient way of increasing his reading vocabulary is to read aloud to him as much as possible, making sure that he can watch the print. (See Chapter 4, III.) This is more difficult to achieve with a roomful of children than with one or two, but since it is so effective, it is worth going to some trouble to make it possible. One way of doing it is to buy sets of interesting, well-illustrated books. Then each child follows in his own book while the teacher reads. Sometimes the children can share the books in pairs, so that partners can point out words to each other as the story goes along. There are bound to be questions like 'Where is that word you just said, Miss?' and the teacher should answer as many of these as she can without holding up the story too much.

By now the children have probably learned most of the sound-names for the letters of the alphabet, by asking questions; but the sounds for the alphabet and combinations can be taught explicitly at this point.

A page by page Book of Phonics is helpful. Each child can be given one or even two pages a day. The capital letter and ordinary letter are printed at the top of the page in red, and a word beginning with the letter is printed at the bottom, twice: once with the capital letter and once with the small one. The beginning letter is again printed in red, and the rest of the word in black or some other colour. This helps a child to pick out the letter in the word.

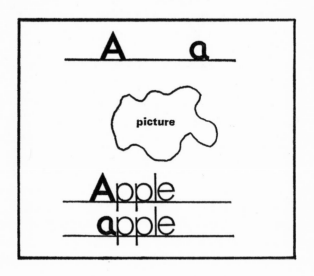

The space in between is for the child's own illustration. He can find a picture of an apple in a magazine, cut it out and glue it in. Or the teacher can draw an outline for him, which he colours, cuts out and pastes in. Or he can draw and colour his own picture. It is a good idea for this to be done on a separate piece of paper so that a messy first attempt does not spoil the book. Children will enjoy learning to use scissors and glue properly so that their very own books look as attractive as possible. Mothers can be encouraged to help their children illustrate the books at home.

The same layout can be used for the combinations:

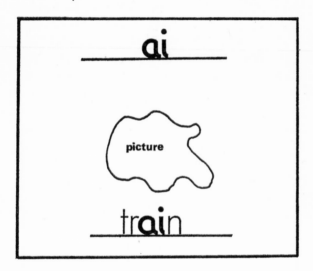

As before, the combination should be red each time, and the other letters black. Nouns which can be easily illustrated should be chosen for the combinations. (See Appendix.)

Printing letters and words on such pages for forty children is again a very different matter from making pages for one or two. Perhaps children in higher classes could undertake this job as well, if the teacher does not have enough time. 'Children power' is a resource we have scarcely tapped as yet.

It is a good idea for a child to build his Book of Phonics backwards, clipping each new page in on top of the old ones, rather than behind them. Then when he is going through his book, he gives his first and freshest attention to the shapes he has learned most recently. The teacher can stop such a session when the child reaches the pages he is really certain of, and before he gets bored.

When going through this book with a child, the teacher should ask him to read the word at the bottom of the page first. Then she covers up the black letters in the word and asks him to pronounce just the letter or combination, saying it for him if he has difficulty. Then she asks him to say the letter or combination at the top of the page, again helping him if necessary. When the child has worked through a few pages in this way, it is helpful to riffle quickly through them once more, asking him to pronounce just the shape at the top of the page, or even saying it for him as he watches. If this is done quickly it isn't tedious, and helps to fix the correct associations in the child's mind.

The class can now play the game of 'spot the sound', seeing who can spot the most sounds in words he can already read.

Once all the shape-sounds have been covered, big charts with all the capitals and lower-case letters, and all the combinations, should go up on the walls, so that the children can look at them any time they wish.

When a child is learning to pronounce the letters and combinations from lists on the blackboard or wall chart, the teacher pronounces each shape herself to begin with, encouraging the child to repeat the sound and point to the shape as he does so. After this, it is again helpful to say: 'Show me "ay". Now show me "ee". Show me "ow". Show me another "ou",' pointing to the shape each time, if the child cannot locate it. Once he is fairly certain of the sounds for the shapes, he can be encouraged to run through them without help from the teacher. The children can work in pairs or groups on this, helping each other.

Whenever a child asks about a particular letter or combination, the teacher should remind him of the sound it makes straight away, without trying to persuade him to think of it himself. (If he could remember it, he wouldn't have asked.) Similarly, if a child makes a mistake, the teacher should usually correct him straight away, without asking him to try again. The children will learn much more quickly if this is done. 'Problems' are for the maths class, not for language.

This sort of approach means that there is no such thing as failure. The child is learning all the time, always receiving just the amount of help he needs to form the proper associations. He is left at the end of each lesson with a confident feeling of knowing, rather than a sense of confusion. After working through the shapes regularly for a few weeks, the child simply finds that the sound for each shape has become second nature to him.

The ability to translate words phonetically should be regarded as a separate skill from reading, and taught thoroughly, as I have indicated. But lessons in phonetics should now become part of the reading lessons, and will take the form of playing the building game with words which are familiar to all the children. The teacher should play the game *with* the children, until they have learned how. The whole class can learn to play by analysing the 12 two-letter words and 30 three-letter words I have listed in Chapter 4, II.

The advantage of using these words is that, being Key Words, they will probably be familiar to the children whatever books happen to have been read, and so offer a systematic approach without tying down the class to any particular series of school readers.

Even though the main line of progress is from two-letter words to three-letter ones and on from there, the teacher can add challenge, from the beginning, by asking who wants her help to play the game with the *longest* word he can read.

This gradual blending in of phonetic translation ensures that there is no jolt for the children, no abrupt transition from seeing words mainly as symbols to seeing them also as collections of shape-sounds. Words which have hitherto been windows on meaning are not suddenly transformed into problems to be solved. There is little likelihood that any child will become confused, but if he does stick at a particular word, all the teacher needs to do is to read it for him first, so helping him to see it as a symbol, and then show him how to fit the sounds to the letters. If reassurance and help are freely available in the early stages, even an apparently 'slow' child will soon gather confidence in his ability to see words both ways by himself.

When reading and phonetics are taught in this natural way, there should be no difficulty about fitting in the children who are already fluent readers when they enter school. I think it would be a pity to regard these children as a group on their own, to be 'creamed off' or isolated while the teacher works with the non-readers. They will be more use – and learn more themselves – if the teacher puts them to work as a growing army of assistant teachers.

A reader can be paired with a non-reader, particularly a non-reader whose mother is unable or unwilling to help him at home. The pair will go through word cards every day, and take turns at reading favourite books to each other. The teacher will need to show her assistants how best to help. (A good teacher will be able to avoid the impression that helping someone else to read is more important than helping someone to play marbles, or make a paper bird, or get to the top of the climbing frame. Every child has abilities which the rest of the group can be encouraged to use and appreciate.) If a reader can write as well as read, his partner can be asked to make up a story while the 'scribe' writes it down, with help from the teacher to make sure that simple sentences are used. Here, making up the story is obviously more important than just writing it out, and the 'author' can be the one who illustrates the book. 'You make such exciting pictures, Janet—you draw pictures for your book, will you, so we can all see the way it was inside your head.'

When should school children learn to write?

Learning to read and learning to write now go hand in hand, but this may well be a mistake. It is much easier to understand language than it is to reproduce it. A baby who is learning to talk can understand far more than he can say, and in just the same way a school child should be able to read easily before he is taught to write. At the moment, we assume that writing aids a child's early attempts to read. It is more likely that it is a hindrance, for making the letters himself will interfere with a child's efforts to perceive words as unified wholes. Before he is ready to learn phonetics, learning to construct individual letters will probably slow down his reading. Nor is writing the best way of learning to associate letters with sounds, when phonetics are introduced. It is easier for a child to learn to associate letters with sounds, by picking out letters in words he can already read.

I suggest that beginning readers should be allowed to

9

trace over whole words if they want to, but organized attempts to teach them to write should be postponed until they are reading fluently. At this point, learning to write should be more rapid and enjoyable anyway.

Instead of being discouraged from helping, parents should be specifically asked to help a child with his reading at home. Their help will often make all the difference to his progress. There are three main reasons for this, quite apart from the child's pleasure in their encouragement.

First, no child really learns to read during a reading lesson. He learns to read on his own, when he picks up a book and goes through it just because he wants to. A mother knows her child's particular interests, and buys for him the books that *he* will most enjoy. It is easier for her than for a teacher to make these books available in relaxed conditions, where the child can pick and choose as he pleases, read when he pleases, stop reading when he pleases. Second, a child who is learning to read needs regular individual help, which it is not always possible for a teacher to give. Third, a child learns better if his 'lessons' are spaced, in short amounts, through the day. If he does no reading at home, he is more likely to have forgotten Tuesday's words by the time he gets back to school on Wednesday.

So the school could request a mother to go through five to ten word cards with her child each day, reading these for him if he has difficulty. When a child starts on books, his mother should be asked to hear all his pages every day, sharing his pride as each new page is added. Again, she should help by reminding her child of words he may have forgotten. This will take a mother no more than about five minutes a day. She can also be asked to read aloud to her child, using books with good clear print for the child to watch as she reads. She can be asked to point out a word whenever the child asks about it, repeating it clearly and explaining its meaning if necessary. She can be asked to answer the child's questions about individual letters, using sound-names; to go through his *Book of Phonics* with him, and to play the building game with old words and new ones when the child is learning phonetic translation. She should be asked not to make a child work out the sound for a word by himself if he finds this difficult.

A few circulars to explain the school's approach, and a few P.T.A. meetings to discuss it, will succeed in involving many parents.

In cases where a mother cannot help, this is such a serious disadvantage that a teacher should try to make up for it by appointing another child to help instead—either an older child, or, as I have suggested, a reader in the same class as the beginner.

The use of written language in the classroom can now branch out in all directions at once. Now the aim should be to surround the children with written language as freely and as meaningfully as they are surrounded with speech. Sentences can be written as they are said, and read aloud once more to make their meaning plain. New words can be pointed out and built up phonetically by the teacher, with the children copying her. The children can be asked to follow any stories—even quite complicated ones—which the teacher reads aloud. Again, some new words can be pointed out when the story is finished, and built up phonetically. In addition, the children should be making steady individual reading progress. If they are not, then in all likelihood the print is too small, or the books are just plain dull.

Formal testing? What is that? Failure? There is no such word. Pressure? Who has been pressured?

The children have been *taught, shown, helped.*

'Reading ages'? As sensible as 'understanding ages'; for it is the level of a child's *understanding* which should now dictate the choice of books for him to read.

How long should it take before the gap between hearing language and seeing it is closed for our school children? Let us aim at one year, instead of three or four.

# 10

## When Reading Comes First: Teaching English as an Unfamiliar Language

The blinkers come off. We realize that a child does not have to understand speech before we begin helping him to read. Into the light of the new idea answers to some of our toughest educational problems begin to emerge, one by one.

Children who don't know any English, or very little, when they start primary school in England, are a problem. Before we can even begin teaching them to read, we have to set to and teach them spoken English.

If Doman is right, we should teach them to see, hear and speak English all at the same time. We have assumed that understanding speech is easy, reading is hard. Yet Doman thinks that seeing language is even easier than hearing it, and he may well be right.

Written language does have two definite advantages over spoken language. The gaps between words are clearer on the page—normal speech runs them together without a break—so that written words are easier to distinguish from one another. And a child can stop and look at a particular word for as long as he wishes, whereas a spoken word which has not been understood is lost to the ears until someone uses it again.

So it is logical to suppose that a child who is learning a

foreign language finds the shape-word easier to distinguish and 'hold on to' than the sound, and can learn the spoken word by linking it with the shape.

Renu and Anita are Hindi-speaking Indian children, daughters of another teacher at the school in Tanzania where we live. Their mother uses hardly any English; their father knows English quite well, but has not used it with the children. Renu, at five, is old enough to begin school, but there are no suitable schools near enough. Anita is four.

I couldn't offer to help the children to read Hindi, for there were hardly any Hindi books and materials available. Also, as a mere adult, I felt quite unable to master their language. So I offered to help them to read mine. Their parents were pleased with the idea, and Mr Garg said the children would go to an English medium school when the family returned to India.

I lent him my tattered copy of *Teach Your Baby To Read*, and explained exactly what I would do. I asked him to help, for Renu and Anita would be coming to 'school' only three times a week. They would really learn to *read* at home. My job would be to plan their programme, make word cards, choose books, and set them going.

I began with the children's own names on large word cards, and words Scotch-Taped on tables, chairs, windows and pictures around the room. I was not very concerned with getting them to *say* all these words. I wanted to show them what words are: that these odd squiggles on bits of card could convey *meanings*. I banged the table, pointed to the card sticking to it, and said 'table'. Then, to my own daughter Gwynneth: 'Where is "table"?' Gwynneth obliged by banging the table and pointing to the card. Renu and Anita soon got the idea and joined in with the table thumping and card pointing when I said: 'Where is "table"?'

After this work with word cards, we moved on to books. We relied on Ladybird books mainly. I chose several books from the 'Learning To Read' series (*Puppies and Kittens, The Farm, The Zoo, Shopping with Mother*, etc.) for Renu and Anita to read at home, and the first three books from the Ladybird Key Words Reading Scheme, for them to read with me.

Because this reading scheme is so carefully planned, it is most helpful for children who are making a beginning with English, as well as reading. The meanings for the first words introduced can be learned from the illustrations, and these same words, together with further illustrations, provide the context which builds up the meanings for later words. (I have one reservation about the scheme. The written material is a bit dull, and Peter and Jane are too nice, too well-mannered, too clean and too neatly dressed! But the illustrations are colourful and enticing. The idea behind the scheme is very sound, and new words are so well presented, their meanings so carefully built up, that I would not hesitate to use the books with any child learning to read English. Of course, I would use plenty of other books with him as well.)

I read the books aloud to Renu and Anita, pointing to the illustrations and then to each word, encouraging the children to repeat the word after me. In this way, the sounds were associated with the written words and with their meanings. I then read the sentence aloud once more, to give the children an ear for the flow and movement of English speech.

The conventional roles of written and spoken language were reversed: I was using reading to help speech, rather than vice versa.

Once a new word had been introduced in its written form, I used it frequently in speech while the children played: 'Renu *and* Anita'; 'Helen *and* Gwynneth'; '*Here is a* doll'; '*Here is a* ball'; '*Here is*—?' Gradually, words which had been presented in this way began to emerge in the children's speaking vocabularies.

We tackled Books 2a, 3a and 4a in the Key Words Scheme in a similar fashion. I began putting words on the blackboard to help Renu and Anita recognize them out of context. When we were halfway through 3a, we began the alphabet. Renu and Anita had read some other books at home by this time, and had a reading vocabulary of about 70 words.

Each child built her own Book of Phonics as I have described in Chapter 9. I discovered these were more practical than cards for carrying back and forth between home and 'school'. And children of school age enjoy helping to make their own books. The words for the letters were taken mainly from John Burningham's *ABC*, and I often went through this book with Renu and Anita, so helping them to learn the meanings of the words from the pictures. (I substituted 'ink' for 'iguana' and 'x-ray' for 'xylophone'.) For the combinations, I chose words which could be easily illustrated and which represented objects within their everyday experience. I put letters and combinations on the blackboard as the children learned them, and left them up.

As we embarked on each new stage, I explained to Mr Garg exactly what I was doing, and how he could take part. This helped a great deal. Each time Renu and Anita returned to 'school', they knew all the material I had given them the time before. Occasionally Mr Garg was too busy to help, and the difference was immediately noticeable.

As we moved on to other books, I chose ones written in

rhyme: *Ten Apples Up On Top* and *My Big Golden Counting Book*. Children are attracted by rhyme (perhaps more beginning reading books could use it) and it is very helpful when they are learning phonetics. *Ten Apples Up On Top*, for example, can provide enjoyable practice in linking sounds with mop, drop, stop, hop, top; three, see, tree; down, town; let, get; and so on. If the teacher introduces the building game later, she can go back to these words and the children will find it very easy to learn to build their sounds.

*My Big Golden Counting Book* has tempting illustrations and a more sophisticated text. (Words like 'proud', 'because', 'each', 'sniffs', 'waddling', 'swish', 'swimming', 'brook', 'shape', 'wild' are used.) I felt that the context would be sufficient to build up the beginnings of meanings for these words, at any rate. There is a picture of a certain number of objects, mostly animals, on each page, and a verse to go with the picture. I went through the book first with a marking pen and printed the name of each object on the picture in big letters. The children began the book by learning just these names, both written and spoken, linking them with the pictures. Then I pointed out these words in the text and a few other words whose meanings could be made clear from the pictures. After a while I read the verses aloud, pointing to each word as I went along.

Now I began helping the children to read the book themselves, word by word. I put up a certain number of words on the blackboard for each lesson, read them aloud to the children, and tried to make their meanings clearer by using them in other spoken sentences, made up of words Renu and Anita could already understand. The children practised pronouncing these words from the blackboard, and then read aloud a few verses from the book. Again,

I continued to use the words in meaningful speech to the children after they had been presented in this way.

After about six months, Renu and Anita had read the following books with me: 1a, 2a, 3a and 4a in the Key Words Scheme, John Burningham's *ABC*, *Ten Apples Up On Top*, *Puppies and Kittens* and *My Big Golden Counting Book*. They had a reading vocabulary of about 300 words, knew all the sounds for the letters and combinations, and had learned to analyse the 12 two-letter words and 30 three-letter words listed in Chapter 4, II. At this point, our first tour at the school in Tanzania ended, and I left their father with a list of books and suggestions for helping them further with phonetic translation.

From this, I am quite certain that non-English-speaking children in British primary schools who are helped to read and hear English at the same time will master the language much more quickly than if their reading is delayed. We should also note that when English-speaking children learn a foreign language in primary school, they should learn both to read and speak it from the beginning.

Can the non-English-speaking parents help their children? Not very much, but in this case I suggest that once again the conventional roles should be reversed, and the children should teach their parents English. (If there are small brothers and sisters in the home, the school child can teach them too.) The child should be encouraged to read to his parents every day, pointing out the words and trying to explain their meanings. This will still give a child the regular reading practice that he needs, and with the added incentive of wanting to help the family he will make an extra effort to learn the meanings of the words at school. Teachers should try to explain to the parents that daily reading will help both the children and themselves, and how they can help the children.

I suggest that an older child from an English home who reads well should be appointed as 'reading partner' for each non-English-speaking child. His job will be to help the other child at school, and also to visit his home and show the parents how to tackle 'reading lessons'. If he picks up a foreign language himself in the process, this will be an added dividend. He could be encouraged to learn about the family's customs and culture, and contribute valuable information to class discussions.

This sort of programme will not only help the non-English-speaking children to learn to read, but should also help to integrate both children and parents into the English-speaking community. And the immigrant parents will be less likely to feel that their children are growing away from them into a world where they cannot follow.

**PART FOUR**

The Ways We Think

# 11

## Patterns of Thinking: a Summing Up

New ideas reveal new patterns. The elements in the pattern were always there. But a sudden hoist of the kaleidoscope shows similarities where none were thought to exist. The moon is like an apple and the earth pulls both. Seeing new similarities, we are obliged to act in new ways. The new patterns eventually change our ideas.

Reading is like hearing, and a baby can be master of both.

There are basic patterns in our thinking, and if we examine these patterns closely, perhaps we shall be able to be more confident in our response to the beginnings of childish, intelligent thought.

Readin', writin', and 'rithmetic. The world of written language and the world of numbers: the main areas, we believe, of intellectual development. We have supposed that a child who is at home in these worlds has progressed a long way.

Yet it seems to me that once we start paying real attention to what lies behind an ordinary baby's ability to hear and to speak, we shall come to see that a speaking baby has already perfected all the basic mental processes, and that before he is well out of the crib!

## I. Basic mental processes

A baby absorbs, with greedy hunger, an enormous amount
of stimuli: sights, sounds, smells, tastes, sensations. From this
chaos of sense impressions, he draws order, forming associations, noticing similarities, fitting together separate pieces
of the jigsaw puzzle. Before long, stray bits of sense data
are no longer perceived in and for themselves: they assume
meanings because of their associations with other sense
data. The clinking of plates and a bib tied under the chin
mean food. Putting on warm clothes means a ride in the
pram.

This kind of interpretation of sense data is a matter of pure
association. Two things are simply linked in the mind, and
either one can signify the other. In technical language, when
one is the sign, the other is the object signified, and vice versa.
The interpretation of such signs is the simplest form of intelligence, and is shared with humans by animals. Pavlov's dog,
learning to salivate in response to the ringing of a bell, a
*sign* that food is coming, is demonstrating this form of
intelligence.

But human beings possess a further kind of intelligence
which has made possible the whole panorama of human
history. They can not only fasten upon various sense data
and use them as signs: they can also use them as symbols. The
formation of sounds which a baby hears as a symbol for his
concept of 'cup-ness' is not identified with any particular
cup, as a sign would be. It stands for a highly abstract
idea.*

A baby's developing mental life centres around these two
ways of interpreting sense data. When he learns to hear language, he is learning to interpret symbols, and when he

* See *Philosophy in a New Key*, by Susanne Langer, pp. 53–64.

learns to speak, as I shall show in a minute, he is learning to associate signs and objects.

## II. How language works

Because spoken words are so much more convenient to use than written words, almost all babies learn to understand speech long before they learn to read. As a result, we have identified language with the understanding and reproduction of sounds. But why is it that a sound can function as a word? Not, logically, *because* it is a sound, but because it can be perceived by one of the senses, and be distinguished as an entity. Not because it is a sound, but simply because it is a *sense datum*.

A shape is no less a sense datum than a sound; therefore there is no logical reason for supposing that it cannot function in the same way.

We think of spoken language as natural, 'given'; and of written language as artificially constructed, shape by shape. But a spoken word is also an artificial invention, a pattern of sounds deliberately selected by human beings from the comparatively small number of basic sounds available to the human voice.

Although a written word is exactly comparable to a spoken word, a new logical element was introduced when human beings invented writing, something which had not existed at all when there was only speech, because it could not. This new element was the *relationship* between the two forms of language, and it is this relationship which has caused most of the problems and confusion about reading. We knew that a written word was invented to represent a sound. A spoken word meant what it meant. So we found it difficult to see that the forms of the two kinds of word were logically identical. What we did not see is that a written word also 'means what it means', and that when a written word signifies a sound, *that sound signifies the shape in exactly the same way*. If a child did not learn to visualize a shape in response to a sound, he would never be able to *write* a word he *hears*. 'Subvisualization' is a common mental occurrence exactly comparable to 'subvocalization', although it usually takes place just below the level of conscious awareness. We are often less aware of the corresponding sounds for written words than we suppose. When we read quickly, we concentrate on what we are reading *about*. But we are aware of subvocalization if we try to catch ourselves *not* thinking of the sounds for the words! Make the switch: try to be conscious of yourself listening to a speaker *without* 'seeing' his words, and you may find that forming the mental image of a word is one of the responses your own mind makes to the spoken word.

In spite of the connection between written and spoken words, Dr Doman maintains that teaching phonetics is unnatural, 'because we don't teach a child to hear language phonetically, so why should we teach him to see language phonetically?' It is quite true that a child does not need to know phonetics in order to understand speech. But we *do* teach him to hear language phonetically, at the exact same time that we teach him to see language phonetically. We cannot teach him to analyse a written word by saying 'bu, ba, bad' without teaching him to analyse the equivalent spoken word at the very same moment. When he points to a 'b' and says 'bu', he is responding to a shape by producing a sound. When we say 'bu' and he points to the letter 'b', he is responding to the sound by identifying the shape. We teach him to 'see sounds', but we cannot do this without also teaching him to 'hear shapes'.

A child who could read, but who did not need to speak

or understand speech, would have no need of phonetics, just as a child who can hear but not read does not need to know phonetics.

Although the relationship between written and spoken language cannot exist for a child until he has experienced both forms to some degree, he *has* had experience of a comparable relationship, usually long before he learns to read. This is the relationship between heard language and uttered language. The relationship happens so naturally for hearing people that we have hardly recognized that there is a distinction between uttering words and hearing the words we say.

But producing the sound 'mu', for example, provides a definite sensation which is distinct from that of producing the sound 'cu' or 'a', and distinct from the separate sensation of hearing the sound produced. We can also *feel* the difference between uttering a sound and merely going through the silent motions with the mouth alone. We could call the feeling of uttering a particular sound a 'vocal sensation'. No less than a sound or a shape, it is a sense datum.

To begin with, a baby doesn't *know* what sound he will produce when he plays with his voice in a certain way. It is only gradually that he learns to associate the sound he makes with the sensation he experiences when he is producing that sound, so that he can make the sound deliberately. When he can produce the sound 'mu' at will, he has learned to associate one sense datum (a sound) with another sense datum (a vocal sensation), so that he can think of one, and translate it into the other. He is linking *signs* with *objects*.

Of course he does not limit himself to single sounds. He moves his lips in a succession of 'mu's. Or he finishes the 'mu' sound with his tongue against his palate, and says 'mud'.

The complex sound 'mud' is then associated, as a whole, with the complex sensations of producing it.

The baby becomes aware that there are other sounds coming to him, sounds which he is not making but which are familiar because they are like the sounds he makes. Some are simple sounds, which he can reproduce easily. Others are complex, and if he has not yet chanced to make them, he learns to analyse them into their constituent sounds, fitting the corresponding vocal sensation to each sound, and combining these sensations to produce a unified utterance, just as the complex sound itself is a unit.

The pattern is the exact same pattern which a child follows when he learns to translate written language into spoken language. First, he learns to associate simple shapes (single letters) and complex shapes (groups of letters) with their corresponding sounds. Then he learns to analyse a written word into its constituent parts, fitting the corresponding sound to each part and combining these sounds to make a word just as the letters are combined to make a word.

I believe that this recognition of the logical similarity between learning to speak and learning phonetics can be very helpful in one or two important areas. It can help us to teach phonetics to hearing children, because once we have analysed how they learn to translate heard language into uttered language, we can duplicate the same pattern when we are helping them to translate written language into spoken language.

Although the two relationships are logically identical, a child usually finds learning to speak much easier than learning phonetics, because he *cannot* produce a sound separately from the feeling of uttering it. He cannot help but learn to associate the two. Before he utters his first consciously meaningful word, he has made hundreds of these

associations. He has combined sounds and their corresponding sensations in any number of ways to form scores of
varied vocables, all with the greatest of ease and a huge
sense of satisfaction in his prowess. Some of his vocables
happen to be words, but he does not know it yet.

Quite apart from this babbling process, the baby has been
learning to understand spoken language. Gradually he fits
the two together. He realizes that the sound 'mumma', say,
which means his mother, is also a sound that he has made.
He has already formed the association between hearing the
sound and making it, so he has no difficulty in imitating the
word when it comes to him from his mother. But his
mother's word comes to him charged with meaning, and the
baby now endows his own utterance with the same meaning.
He is not just babbling any longer. He is *speaking*. Once
reproducing *words* is an exciting game, he can analyse many
different heard words and translate them into vocal sensation
words. The process of analysis and translation is easy and
rapid, because of the large store of simple and complex associations which he has already made. No effort of memory,
no laborious, conscious struggle to analyse is needed.

When we stop assuming that such a struggle is inherently
virtuous, and concentrate on *providing* for our children the
association between letters and sounds, and the phonetic
analysis of written words, as frequently as need be, until
they have built up a similarly large store of associations, then
I maintain that they will learn phonetics as easily as they
learned to speak. The association between letters and sounds
does not happen naturally and inevitably, so we must make
it happen. A mother playing the building game *for* her child
is helping him to associate a great number of signs (sets of
letters) with their objects (corresponding sounds). Each time
she uncovers a letter, her child sees a different set of letters as

a whole, and associates that set with one sound unit. For example, when a mother uncovers the word 'basket', letter by letter, her child learns to associate, not *one* set of letters ('basket') with its sound, but *six* sets ('b', 'ba', 'bas', 'bask', 'baske', 'basket'). Sets like this recur in many different words, and the child can translate each set at a glance whenever he sees it, *because he has already learned to do so*. This is why he moves so swiftly from the building game to the point where he can translate unfamiliar words at sight, without bothering to cover them up. Their basic patterns are already thoroughly familiar, and he needs to take note only of the slight differences in sound arrangement.

We must also recognize that understanding written language happens quite separately from translating it, and that a child should not be expected to translate written language by himself until he can understand it easily. To begin with, we translate it for him, and we do this to help build up the meanings for the written words. But this translation is also an excellent way of providing the associations between written and spoken words. It is the beginning of teaching phonetics, and is much more enjoyable for a child than if we begin with the alphabet. He starts to form many associations between letters and sounds as he reads aloud exciting, meaningful words. Later on, teaching him 'the alphabet' is simply a matter of clarifying these associations.

At this point, an interesting question emerges about the education of the deaf. Since spoken words can hardly help a totally deaf child to provide written words with meanings, is it necessary—even supposing it were possible—to teach him phonetics?

At first thought, it seems both impossible and unnecessary. But even if a deaf child cannot hear the sounds he makes, he can be aware of the sensations of producing them.

If, whenever we succeed in helping him to produce an identifiable sound, we show him the corresponding letter or group of letters straight away, he will gradually learn to associate that shape with the sensation of producing the sound, *so that after a while he can respond to the shape by uttering the sound.* As we make full use of all the sounds, both simple and complex, which he produces, we can help him to translate a growing number of meaningful written words into uttered sounds. This will indeed have very little to do with helping him to understand written language. *But it can have a great deal to do with helping him to speak.*

In fact very few deaf children have no hearing whatever. Most can hear their own voices when the sounds are amplified by some kind of hearing-aid. In *Teaching Deaf Children To Talk*, by Ewing and Ewing, modern methods of teaching deaf children are described. The Ewings point out that some deaf children can hear certain sounds, but not others with the help of hearing-aids. They can nevertheless be taught to articulate sounds they cannot hear, sometimes by watching their own facial movements in a mirror and matching these to their teachers'. They are also trained to control the flow of breath so as to modify various sounds. When uttered 's', for example, has been learned in this way, the letter is presented as well, until the deaf child can respond to it by producing the uttered sound.* If he can hear his utterance, of course the heard sound is also linked with the same letter. But even when heard sounds are included, the link between the shape and the vocal sensation is still establishing itself independently in the child's mind, and enables him, later, to say written words aloud without having to hear what he says. (A hearing child learning phonetics forms an

* See *Teaching Deaf Children To Talk*, by Ewing and Ewing, pp. 7, 224 and 227.

identical association between letters and vocal sensations, as well as heard sounds, but the link never has to function independently in his case. It is quite possible, though, for a hearing person to read aloud without listening to what he is saying!)

The pronunciation of irregular words can be made clear to a deaf child by linking a word like 'cough' with an exact phonetic rendering. 'Coff' could be printed underneath the word the child can already understand.

The big advantage of teaching phonetics to a deaf child who can read is that he is enabled to link his feelings of utterance with meaningful *words*, as well as with (for the partially hearing) blurred and often still meaningless sounds. The meaning of a written word fuses with the sensation of saying it, and these 'vocal sensation' words can become, for the deaf child, symbols in their own right. They are wholes made up of smaller sensations—tongue against palate, lips coming together and apart, vibration in the throat, expelled breath—just as shape-words are made up of smaller shapes, and sound-words of smaller sounds. The deaf child can grow aware of the meaning flowing through his utterance, just as we 'feel' the meaning of the words we say.

A method of teaching deaf children, by combining training in listening and speaking with reading, has been developed by Lady E. C. Ewing, and is described in *Teaching Deaf Children To Talk*.* It has proved extremely helpful, but it does not seem to have been used with children below the age of five. Once we have recognized how natural and easy reading is, and how closely the phonetic translation of written words mimics the reproduction of spoken words, I feel sure that Lady Ewing's method will be used successfully with much younger deaf children.

* Op. cit., pp. 162–78.

I see the three forms of language making a pattern as follows: if a child can understand a spoken word, and nothing more, he hears the spoken word in one way only: as the symbol of an idea. As he learns to speak, that word summons up *two* distinct and separate associations in his mind. It summons up an idea and he understands it. It also summons up the imagined feeling of saying it, and he can, if he wishes, utter it. When he can also read that word, the spoken word summons up *three* associations: an idea, the feeling of saying it and the corresponding shape. A child's conscious awareness of any one of these associations varies with the purpose for which he happens to be listening.

This process operates in reverse, and a written word summons up three comparable associations: an idea, the feeling of saying it and the corresponding sound:

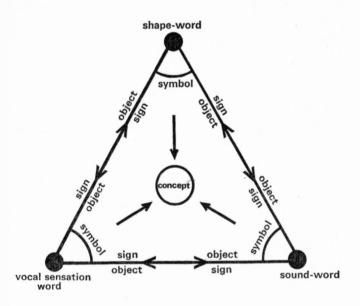

So we can see that a written word functions exactly like a spoken word.★

## III. Language and mathematics

The educational advance signalled by Doman's insight into the workings of written language results from a shift in theoretical thinking. Doman asked himself, not: 'What does a child have to learn?' but: 'How does he learn it? Does he use the same pattern of thinking in another area?' If the pattern of thinking is identical, then it follows logically that the material can be mastered in the same way. Our task is to make the material itself as vivid and interesting as we can.

This same theoretical shift is providing significant insights in the other, seemingly remote area of intellectual development: the world of mathematics. It is being more clearly recognized that the mental processes underlying language are the same processes which are used in certain mathematical operations: and once again, the logical conclusion is that if a small child can handle the one, he can handle the other.

When, for example, we use the word 'door' with a small child, and he understands us, that word summons up for him an idea which contains all the characteristics of all the doors he has come across. He may have known big doors and little doors, wide doors and narrow doors, stiff doors and gentle doors, doors made entirely of wood and doors with window panes he could see through. Doors that swing vertically and trap-doors to be raised and lowered. All the doors could open

★ This theory of language rests heavily on Susanne Langer's brilliant analysis in *Philosophy in a New Key*. Anyone who is interested in the philosophical underpinnings of my discussion will find Mrs Langer's book most exciting. See particularly her chapters on 'The Logic of Signs and Symbols' and 'Language'. Mrs Langer does not recognize that a written word is a symbol in its own right, but all the implications are there.

and close; someone or something could pass through them all when they were open, but not when they were closed. These characteristics, and more besides, some common to all the doors he knows, some to only one or two, are united for him in the single concept of 'door-ness'.

Now suppose that this same child can approach an object which he has never seen before, and label it unhesitatingly, correctly, 'door'. It might be a red door to a doll's house, with gilt hinges and a wooden knob; and he may never before have seen such a small door with these particular characteristics. What mental processes have gone on enabling him to name this object correctly?

In his previous experience of doors, he has not only stored away a mental impression of all their characteristics: he has also isolated those characteristics which are shared by all the doors. All the doors open and shut; they keep things out or in when they are shut, and can let things through when they are open. The door on the doll's house has these characteristics, and it isn't enclosed by the wall, which could make it a window: so it very probably is a door.

Now let us make one more supposition. The same child comes across another doll's house with a false door in the front. It looks just like the red door with the wooden knob, but when he tests it, he finds that it won't open. It is merely painted on to the front wall of the house. Another child, fooled by appearance, may say: 'Look. There's the door,' but the first replies disgustedly: 'Oh no. It *looks* like a door, but it won't open, so it isn't.' (The second child may not have decided that opening and shutting are essential features of doors, so he may persist in his opinion—also quite logical, according to his premises—that the false door may properly be called one.)

If we didn't take this kind of childish thinking for granted so readily, we might be more impressed by the intellectual operations involved. Seton Pollock, in his book *The Basic Colour Factor Guide*, points out that this pattern of thinking is the exact same pattern followed by a mathematician when he arrives at the lowest common multiple and the highest common factor of a set of factors:

> We are apt to suppose that these procedures are entirely new and unfamiliar to the pupils to whom they are taught, but they are, in fact, a special application of mental processes which were developed in early infancy when learning to understand and use speech. When we use a common noun, the idea it summons up contains all the characteristics of all the objects that can bear that name. It is an 'L.C.M.'. Moreover, to come to that idea, and to be capable of giving it a name, we must be able to extract from all those objects, which may be surprisingly different from one another, the element or elements that are to be found in each one of them. The noun is an 'H.C.F.', also. (p. 214)

Elsewhere in the book, Mr Pollock points out that the processes by which we extract an H.C.F. and an L.C.M.

> are not addition, subtraction, multiplication or division. Any or all of these so-called basic processes may be involved, and multiplication is always involved; but these new processes have something about them which sets them apart. They are, in fact, operations upon *sets* of factors, and the mathematician is aware that they lead towards the territory opened up by such mathematicians as Boole and Cantor, and the other pioneers in the modern approach to mathematics. (p. 113)

Operations on sets extend far beyond mathematics, and lie at the heart of logical thinking. Although the form of the following syllogism would be strange to the child who rejects the false door, he has already mastered the thinking behind it:

> All doors open and shut.
> This object does not open and shut.
> Therefore, this object is not a door.

In order to reach this conclusion, the child has carried out some quite complex operations on *sets* of characteristics shared by doors.

When I needed a term for a group of letters, the word 'set' was not a haphazard choice. It is a much more precise word than 'group'. A set can contain one object, many objects, or none: a set of letters can include one letter, or many. The important feature of a set of letters is that it is a *whole*, a *unit*, and a child sees it as such. One letter is a unit. Several letters, combined to form a syllable or a word, are equally a unit. Likewise one sound is a unit or set. Several sounds, combined to form a syllable or a word, are equally a set. Various sets can be combined and compared to form new sets (which, once again, are units), and a child is comparing and combining in just this way when he reproduces a spoken word, and when he translates an unfamiliar written word into sounds.

Another thread running through the fabric of both mathematics and language is the idea of ratio. Again, this seems quite a sophisticated concept, yet a child who is fascinated by the idea that Grandpa is Daddy's Daddy has already formed it: Grandpa is to Daddy as Daddy is to him.

Mr Pollock sums up beautifully what I am trying to say

about the connections between mathematical and other kinds of thinking:

> The modern mathematician is interested in these connections, and likes to find ways in which the principles and laws which he discovers in his own field can be applied in others which, at first sight, seem to have nothing to do with mathematics at all ... It does no harm for the teacher to be aware that there is far more in the simplest topics being taught than has ever been supposed; and that the children themselves have a built-in equipment to help them which has already enabled them to perform intellectual prodigies that would be incredible were they not so familiar ... Our intellectual life, in all its aspects, rests upon the ability to abstract elements and to deal with them in pairs and in sets by the processes of combining, ordering and comparing. It is no accident that the word *rationality* is rooted in the conception of *ratio*. (p. 215)

If the thinking behind many mathematical operations is the same as the thinking behind language, why is it that a child usually has so little trouble with language, and so much trouble with maths? The sole difference, surely, lies in the materials through which the thinking is done. A door is very concretely *there*: a child can bang it, rattle it, swing it as much as he pleases, thinking 'door' as he does so. The symbol is associated with a vivid, tangible and interesting object. The names for such objects build up a definite context which, later on, helps to provide the meaning for other parts of speech like 'but', 'when', 'will be', etc. But the symbol '3' is associated only with an abstraction which cannot be smelt, seen, heard, tasted or felt. The symbol itself is the only means available to many children of holding on to the idea of 'three-ness'.

The solution lies in providing materials which will do for numbers what concrete experience does for language, and the Colour Factor Set developed by Mr Pollock does precisely this. (It has much in common with the Cuisenaire rods, but the colour sequence of the Colour Factor Set clarifies certain ideas which are only hazily conveyed by other models.) A child who uses a Colour Factor Set can not only think about 'three' – he can *see* that idea, feel it, bite it, and arrange it in all sorts of patterns or contexts which help to make its meaning clear. And Mr Pollock has discovered that small children who use the Set are capable of seemingly amazing mathematical feats, just as Dr Doman found out that small children who are exposed to large and interesting written words in conjunction with concrete objects can, astonishingly, learn to read.

## IV. The road ahead

What emerges from all this? The main point, I think, is that we must stop regarding a small child who is at home in the world of written language and the world of numbers as some kind of freak, a prodigy who has been deprived of his childhood and forced into intellectual achievements beyond his years. He is merely an ordinary child who has been encouraged to exercise his native mental powers over a wider area than most other children of his age.

Should we, then, open these worlds to a tiny child, or should we leave him to the beads and rattles which have been thought appropriate to his immaturity? And if we choose to give him more than this to exercise his mind – why? Because we want to give him a start in the 'academic rat race'? – surely a meaningless struggle.

I believe that a tiny child has the right to enter these worlds, if for no other reason than that he, like me, gains enormous pleasure just from seeing the patterns in things.

# Bibliography

Sylvia Ashton-Warner, *Teacher* (Penguin, Harmondsworth, 1966)

Lindley C. Boyer, *Who Are You?* (Cape, London, 1965)
*Who Am I?* (Cape, London, 1965)

John Burningham, *ABC* (Cape, London, 1964)

Glenn Doman, *Teach Your Baby to Read* (Cape, London, 1965)
*Nose is Not Toes* (Cape, London, 1965)

Dr Engelmann, *Give Your Child a Superior Mind* (Frewin, London, 1968)

Sir A. and Lady C. Ewing, *Teaching Deaf Children to Talk* (Manchester University Press, 1964)

Susanne Langer, *Philosophy in a New Key* (Oxford University Press, 1957)

Seton Pollock, *The Basic Colour Factor Guide* (Heinemann, London, 1965)

*Sunday Times, Success Before Six*

James Thompson, *Educating Your Baby* (Parrish, London, 1967)

Beginners Books Series (Collins, London)
*ABC* (Dr Seuss, 1964)
*Are You My Mother?* (P. D. Eastman, 1962)

*The Cat In the Hat Beginner Book Dictionary* (Dr Seuss, 1965)

*A Fish Out of Water* (Helen Palmer, 1963)

*A Fly Went By* (M. McClintock, 1961)

*Green Eggs and Ham* (Dr Seuss, 1962)

*The King, the Mice and the Cheese* (N. and E. Gurney, 1966)

*Ten Apples Up On Top* (T. Le Sieg, 1967)

Follet Just Beginning to Read Books (Follett Publishing, Chicago)

*The Funny Baby*

*The Three Bears*

*The Three Goats*

*The Three Little Pigs*

Ladybird Key Words Reading Scheme (Wills and Hepworth, Loughborough)

*Play With Us* (W. Murray, 1964)

*Things We Like* (W. Murray, 1964)

*We Have Fun* (W. Murray, 1964)

Ladybird Learning to Read Series (Wills and Hepworth, Loughborough)

*The Farm* (M. E. Gagg, 1958)

*Numbers* (M. E. Gagg, 1959)

*Puppies and Kittens* (M. E. Gagg, 1956)

*Shopping with Mother* (M. E. Gagg, 1958)

*The Zoo* (M. E. Gagg, 1960)

Ladybird Well-Loved Tales Series (Wills and Hepworth)

*The Gingerbread Boy* (V. Southgate, 1966)

*The Little Red Hen* (V. Southgate, 1966)

*The Three Little Pigs* (V. Southgate, 1965)

My Big Golden Counting Book (Golden Press, N.Y., 1957)

# Appendix: Letter Combinations

this section, I have listed several words which contain each combination. (See p. 65.) I have also picked out words which are suitable for illustrating, if you want to draw pictures on the blackboard or help your child to make a Book of Phonics. He will enjoy matching the word with the picture, and recognizing the sound of the combination as you point it out to him.

But it is probably better to use a short, frequently used word to teach each combination to begin with, and these are not always the ones that are easy to illustrate. The ones you could teach first are printed at the head of each list. Each 'teaching' word is a Key Word, as used in the early books of the Ladybird Key Words Reading Scheme, except for 'chin', 'king' and 'phone'.

Make sure that your child can read the 'teaching' word *first*, before teaching him the sound of the combination.

After you have taught each combination, teach the rest of the words if and when they occur in your child's reading. But if he picks up this book, and tries to translate some of the words in the lists of his own accord, there is no harm in that! If he shows interest in some of the words in the lists, help him to find them in *The Cat In The Hat Beginner Book Dictionary.*

**ai**   train

| nail | laid | |
|------|------|--------|
| pail | rain | again |
| sail | pain | afraid |
| tail | paint | |

---

**aw**   saw

paw

| | law | |
|------|------|--------|
| jaw | lawn | **aw**ful |
| raw | fawn | |
| | yawn | |

---

**ay**   say

crayon

| day | pay | away |
|------|------|--------|
| lay | play | always |
| may | gray | today |
| | stay | |

---

**ch**   chin

children

| chick | itch | catch |
|---------|------|---------|
| cheese | much | lunch |
| chair | ouch | watch |
| chase | rich | scratch |
| church | such | ostrich |
| chimney | | teacher |

168

**k**     back

| | | |
|---|---|---|
| kick | pack | neck |
| lick | sack | luck |
| pick | smack | sock |
| sick | black | pocket |
| quick | crack | block |
| brick | | clock |

---

**a**     sea                                      sea

| | | |
|---|---|---|
| | pea | clean |
| eat | tea | cream |
| easy | meat | dream |
| east | read | breathe |
| | seat | teacher |

---

**e**     tree                                      tree

| | | | |
|---|---|---|---|
| see | free | deep | need |
| seed | three | keep | green |
| bee | feed | peep | queen |
| been | feel | sleep | sweep |
| | feet | | street |

---

**er**     her                                      mother

| | | | |
|---|---|---|---|
| after | butter | hammer | sister |
| over | dinner | ladder | brother |
| under | danger | never | teacher |
| water | father | paper | another |
| wonder | flower | pepper | together |
| | camera | | |

---

**ew**   new        Illustration
                    jewel

dew     few

mew     flew     ewe

pew     threw

        knew

---

**ng**   king                    king

ring

sing    hang

wing    rang      long

thing   sang      hungry

bring   angry morning

string  kangaroo

finger

---

**oa**   boat                    boat

oak     soap

coal    soak

coat    float

road

---

**oo**   room                    broom

moo     boot    tooth   igloo

too     food    goose   noodle

zoo     moon    loose   scooter

        soon    school  balloon

        roof kangaroo

---

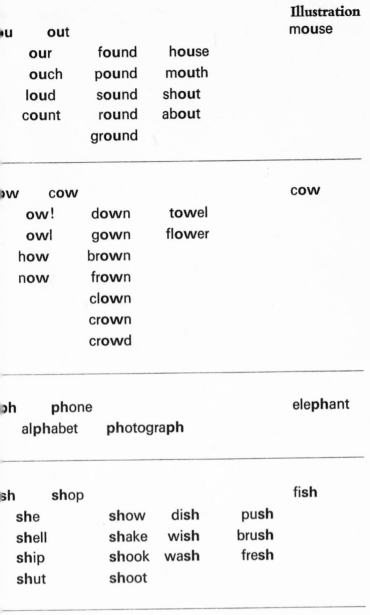

| ou | out | | | mouse |
|---|---|---|---|---|
| | our | found | house | |
| | ouch | pound | mouth | |
| | loud | sound | shout | |
| | count | round | about | |
| | | ground | | |

| ow | cow | | | cow |
|---|---|---|---|---|
| | ow! | down | towel | |
| | owl | gown | flower | |
| | how | brown | | |
| | now | frown | | |
| | | clown | | |
| | | crown | | |
| | | crowd | | |

| ph | phone | | elephant |
|---|---|---|---|
| | alphabet | photograph | |

| sh | shop | | | | fish |
|---|---|---|---|---|---|
| | she | show | dish | push | |
| | shell | shake | wish | brush | |
| | ship | shook | wash | fresh | |
| | shut | shoot | | | |

171

| th | this | | | Illustratio |
|---|---|---|---|---|
| the | | their | with | clothes |
| that | | there | father | |
| them | | these | feather | |
| then | | those | | |
| they | | | | |

---

| wh | when | | | wheel |
|---|---|---|---|---|
| why | | | whale | |
| what | | whisper | while | |
| where | | whisker | white | |
| which | | | | |

---

Not all these words are completely regular as far as their othe sounds go. Your child will usually be able to guess the soun symbols for words with only slight irregularities, if these word are already part of his hearing vocabulary. When he canno teach the sounds without building them up as the words occur and point out the sound made by the combination.

NOTE. Most of the words used as examples in this book are eithe Key Words, as used in the Ladybird Key Words Reading Schem or taken from *The Cat In The Hat Beginner Book Dictionary*, by Dr. Seuss. They are common words which your child will b meeting in his reading very soon.

# DATE DUE
# REMINDER

FEB 21 '99

**Please do not remove
this date due slip.**